Praise for The Rule-Breaker's G

'This book contains the techniques and approach that actually work in social media. Throw out any other guide, because this is all you need to effectively build your brand and business through social media. The best part is that Damian practices what's in this book and he's a true authority worth listening to.'

John Michael Morgan, author of *Brand Against the Machine*

'From the moment I began reading this book I was hooked. It's accessible, funny, down to earth and so informative. I can't wait to start applying the principles and embarking on the 30 Day Challenge. I'm certain it will help propel my business forward.'

Sammie Venn, founder of Soul Warriors Jewellery

'Damian is one of the most inspirational, natural and driven people I have had the pleasure of meeting. I never tire of throwing ideas around with him and getting the benefit of his energy, intelligence, pragmatism and knowledge, which I have seen him use to build businesses, educate, mentor and generally give back to the music industry. Damian always has his sleeves rolled up ready to get stuff done and his infectious personality and experience inspire others to do the same.'

Simon Pringle, CEO of Red River, Business Person of the Year

'Damo is very smart, he has formulated radical new ways of dealing with social media to make sure your content cuts though the noise and reaches your audience in the most effective way. Using his methods we raised £1.2 million to start our new company, WaterBear, and break into a competitive market. Read this book! With this knowledge anything is possible.'

Bruce John Dickinson, Founder Director of WaterBear, Founder Director of BIMM, and member of best-selling band, Little Angels

'Damian continues to be a huge inspiration for me, both professionally and personally. What you see is what you get and the same goes with this book!'

Edward Peter Cox, Managing Director, The Ethical Record Label

'Damian has always been at the very cutting edge of the music industry. His experience, knowledge and insight is unrivalled.'

Mark Clayden, founder of industrial metal band Pitchshifter

THE RULE-BREAKER'S GUIDE TO
SOCIAL MEDIA

DAMIAN KEYES

DK PUBLISHING

30 Brunswick Street East, Hove, BN3 1AU

First published in 2018 by DK Publishing

THE RULE-BREAKER'S GUIDE TO SOCIAL MEDIA.
Copyright © 2018 by Damian Keyes

Printed by Create Space

ISBN 978-1-9996153-0-7

This book is dedicated to my son, Caian. You are my inspiration and my motivation. Every day I wake up ready to work hard and make you proud. Love you, monkey. Thanks for being so awesome. I'm so super proud of you!

'The golden rule is that there are no golden rules.'

George Bernard Shaw

CONTENTS

INTRODUCTION

From the moment we start school – if not sooner – we're taught to obey the rules. Rules like turning up for lessons on time, handing in our homework, and not breaking in at the weekend for the hell of it – or was that just me? Then, when we're sixteen or eighteen or twenty-one, we're churned out on to the conveyor belt, *Another-Brick-in-the-Wall*-style, as obedient little worker-bots ready for a life of industry. But ironically, the most important lesson I ever learned growing up was that, **if you're going to make a success of your life and live it on your own terms, some rules need to be broken**. And never has this been more relevant than today, since the technological revolution that's led to the internet. The irony is, so many of the rules we blindly follow today are no longer relevant. But more of that later. First, let me rewind a little and tell you how my attitude to rule-breaking and business came to be...

Sometimes, when I'm being interviewed, I'm asked for my '*X-Factor* tale' – a tear-jerking account of how I grew up sixteen-to-a-bedroom in a ghetto in Wales, or how I overcame the heartbreak of the death of my hamster aged three. But the truth is, my childhood was pretty much tragedy-free. I grew up in a normal house in a normal, loving family in Swansea. I had my own bedroom and my pets all lived long and happy lives and died peacefully in their sleep. But one thing I can say is that by the time I was nineteen, I'd failed at every single major thing I'd tried to do. And when I say 'failed' I mean failed by the accepted standards fed to us by the system.

My first major failure was my GCSEs (the exams UK students have to take at the age of sixteen). I failed them all. A big factor in that epic failure was that at the age of fifteen I'd fallen madly in love ... with a Silver Ninja. Are you familiar with the Silver Ninja? No, I didn't think so. The Silver Ninja was a bass guitar and I think my mum must have bought the only one in existence for my fifteenth birthday. I'd asked for a bass for my birthday because my best mate and I had decided to start a band. 'You have to play bass though,' my mate told me, 'Because I'm the guitarist.' So that was it, a lifelong love affair was born. I quickly became obsessed with that Silver Ninja and spent hours in my bedroom, playing *Another One Bites the Dust* over and over again. I hadn't realised it at the time but I'd already started breaking the so-called rules – in this case the rule that you have to revise for and pass your GCSEs to have a happy and successful life.

I can remember walking home from school the day I got my results, dreading telling my mum. But she was surprisingly good about it. 'You'll just have to retake the year,' she said. So, while my mates all went on to college, I retook the final year at a different school. And guess what? I failed again. This time it really hurt. Because this time I'd actually tried. I can remember panicking, thinking, *what am I going to do? I'm not cut out for this. Even when I try I don't succeed.* I was also seriously worried that my mum, who had dreams of me becoming a lawyer, was going to go mental. I had to come up with a plan and come up with it fast. By the time I arrived home, I had it. 'Don't worry, Mum,' I told her. 'I've failed my GCSEs a second time but it's all going to be OK because I'm going to be a rock star!'

Somehow, she didn't kill me and I ended up going to a local college to study music on a performing arts course. Around that time I got into a band and we started doing quite well. And by that I mean we got signed to a small, independent label on a 'singles deal'. A singles deal basically did what it said on the tin – the label invested the money for us to record one single and put that single out. The single did quite well and some of the major labels started showing an interest. We did a showcase for Parlophone and signed with them. When the musical equivalent of Manchester United come knocking you don't say no.

So far, so good. Everyone told us we were going to be the next U2, sell millions of records, go on tour and take over the world – all before breakfast. I dropped out of my course, there's no way Adam Clayton would have forfeited world domination for a BTEC in Performing Arts. I was going to be a rock star, which was great because that's what I'd told my mum. We had a manager and an A&R guy – although I'm still not entirely sure what A&R guys do or if they even really exist – and everything was going very well. A lot of money was spent on us recording an album … and then we got shelved. Getting shelved is the music industry equivalent of getting dumped. Only there's no, *'it's not you, it's me'* to soften the blow. When you get shelved by a record label it's *all* you and your label's lack of faith in you. I've since learned that this happens all the time; that record labels will sign a bunch of bands and then wait and see which ones take. But I was only eighteen years old at this point and didn't have a clue how the industry worked. I had total faith in our label. When the musical equivalent of Manchester United come knocking you assume they know what they're doing.

When nothing happened we started getting increasingly anxious that the fan-base we'd grown would forget about us. Eventually, we asked the label to put the album out. They put it out and I think the only person who bought it was my mum. A few weeks later we got dropped from Parlophone. At that point I was nineteen years old. I'd failed my GCSEs twice, I hadn't even got my BTEC because I'd dropped out and now I'd been dumped by a major record label. My plan was not going as well as I'd hoped and I didn't have a clue what to do next. So we sat down with our manager and asked his advice about how we could go about getting signed to another label.

'It's not going to happen,' he said. 'You made the product and you put it out there and it didn't work so that's it, that's the end.' He told us that the only choices we had available to us were to start a new band from scratch or go and get a job. I was staring into the abyss again. Others saw what had happened as a success – at least I'd been signed by a major label – but my dream was over and horribly. The band split up and we all went our separate ways. All of a sudden it was just me against the world and I felt incredibly lonely. I didn't have any back-up plan. The truth is I've got quite an obsessive personality. I believe that if you don't fully commit to something you won't achieve it, so I'm not very good at having a Plan B. Anyone who knows me knows that I've always said, *'fuck plan B'*. I felt very on my own with the whole thing and I didn't know what to do. However, even at my very lowest point thinking, *God, I've got nothing,* I did feel a small spark of excitement, wondering what might come next.

OK, I thought to myself, *I'll go and get a job.* The drummer from our band told me there was a vacancy going in the local shampoo factory where he worked. I applied for the job and got it. I lasted three hours. My job was to stand by a conveyor belt and pick up each bottle of shampoo as it went past and wipe any residual shampoo off the top. That was it, the entire job, wiping shampoo from bottle tops. I told my mate, 'I don't know how long I can do this, it's horrible.' He replied, 'Just bear with it, you get used to it after a while.' It turned out he'd been doing the job for seven years. That prospect was horrifying to me. There was no way I could stay. So I put the shampoo bottle down – wiping it first of course because, standards – and I walked out. Again, without realising it, I was breaking a rule; that you need to 'get used to' unfulfilling work in order to earn a living. As I walked home that day I didn't have a clue what I was going to do next, but what I knew for certain was that I loved to play bass, the only thing I understood was music, and I wanted to build my life around music, so I was just going to have to figure it out. I realised that I needed to learn all about the industry if I was ever going to achieve any kind of success. So I left Swansea and enrolled in a college called ACM in Guildford. It was a very small college, with only forty-four students at the time. I was incredibly lucky because I met some great mentors there, who had a lot of common sense and experience and they taught me so much. One of those mentors was Bruce Dickinson, former guitarist with Little Angels, who'd had a number one album and toured the world with bands like Bon Jovi, ZZ Top, Aerosmith and Guns n' Roses. Bruce was not only the manager of the school but one of the teachers too. He taught subjects like Business Studies and Live Performance. The thing I really liked about him was that he didn't just come in and talk at us, he was completely available, which made such a difference. He also helped me get rid of some seriously unhelpful assumptions I had about the music industry. One of those assumptions was that people often luck out and cheat their way into the industry and real talent isn't always recognised. Bruce once mentioned the band Oasis in an early class and, being a technical musician and a kid, I said, 'Oasis are shit'. Bruce replied, 'It doesn't matter, they've sold 12 million albums so they've definitely done something right, but instead of trying to learn what they've done, you're just dismissing them.'

He was right. The fact is, it's bloody hard to sell a record – let alone 12 million. If a band are selling that amount they're doing something very right. It doesn't matter whether you like them or not, the fact is, they're winning. As soon as Bruce said that and shut me down I thought, *oh God, he's right, this is why I'm not successful.* I realised then that every time Bruce said something I needed to shut up and listen. And I've been doing that every day since for the past twenty years!

There were six other bass players at the college and we had two bass teachers. One left unexpectedly one Christmas, when he decided to go snowboarding and never came back. The other teacher got snowed in at home up in Leicester, so we were told we might as well go home until he was able to get back. I was gutted. I didn't want to go home, I wanted to carry on having fun with my friends and playing bass, so I offered to take the class until the teacher returned. Another so-called rule was being broken – that students can't be teachers – and it paid off big-time. When our teacher returned, the college offered me a part-time job teaching the younger kids in the evening. I had a grand total of three students, plus I was doing any and every odd job the college could think of to give me. Whether it was unblocking toilets, cleaning carpets, picking people up or dropping them off, I didn't care because I was also getting paid to do something I loved. The college grew and I ended up becoming one of the four managers. Then in 2001, Bruce told me that he was leaving. I was crushed. I felt that ACM would be a rudderless ship without him and working there would no longer be any fun. By that point my entire life revolved around one thing – waking up and enjoying the day. I've never been motivated by money. For me, it's all about enjoying what I do and I couldn't see how I'd enjoy ACM without Bruce.

One day, when we were walking to the carpark after work, I asked him what he was going to do next. He said 'I don't know' and I said, 'OK, I'm coming with you.' He said, 'I might go to Scarborough,' and I thought, *well, that's not ideal but I'm still coming with you.* I told him, 'I don't care what I have to do, if I have to clean the toilets or be the runner, I'm coming with you whether you like it or not.' I left him standing in the carpark with a very blank look on his face. He must have thought I was a lunatic! But then a few days later, Bruce told me that he'd had the idea for a new music college and asked if I'd like to help him start it. Obviously I agreed and I was made 25% owner and a founder-director of Brighton Music College, or BIMM, as it would become known. At 23, I was youngest on the team by a good eight years. I was not expecting to be made a director at all. As I said, I'd have been happy being the janitor, but I think Bruce recognised my ability to make things happen and he trusted me with the responsibility.

BIMM was based out of my living room at the start. All four founder-directors would meet there to discuss things. We'd bought a premises but it had to be completely gutted and rebuilt, which took six long months. During that time we kept meeting in my living room and cafes, building the business from scratch. There were some very dark times during that period; times when we'd almost run out of money, or when the competition would try and stop what we were doing, but even so, every day I'd wake up excited. It felt like an adventure; like going into a really dark jungle and even though you're scared it's a good kind of fear because you just don't know what's going to happen.

People would ask us how we could possibly take on and compete with a college the size of ACM. But the reasons these people had for doubting us were exactly the same things that filled me with confidence. As far as I was concerned, ACM couldn't compete with *us*. They might have just had a £2 million investment into their state of the art building, and we might have only had a building site, a charity shop computer and a table, but what we did have was our knowledge and experience and a killer strategy, and that was the secret of what was to become our phenomenal success. Basically, we knew how to help students better than anyone else. And we were going to limit the number of students we took on to ensure we could achieve this.

The college building was still being renovated when we started interviewing potential students for places. We weren't allowed inside for health and safety reasons but we needed to show students where they'd be going. So we'd interview them on a Saturday when the builders weren't there and sneak them inside for a look. We'd explain to them that we weren't allowed to go upstairs because the floor might collapse. It was amazing how quickly our tours would come to an end after that! Then we'd decamp to the café across the road with a notepad and pen and we'd ask the potential student where they were at with their music and where they wanted to go with their career. This is the opposite of what music colleges normally do. They like to focus solely on education but we'd also focus on careers. Everyone who came for an interview with us would leave with a career plan, even if they didn't end up joining us. Nobody in music education sales could do that because they just didn't have the experience we did. To come from nothing and achieve in the music industry is a very specific skill.

In social media terms, we were like the starter vlogger, sitting on their bed, talking into their phone, who turns their channel into a multi-million pound interest. The fact is, you can have all the fancy equipment and production staff in the world but nothing can compete with the real deal. The knowledge that Bruce and I had was real and more importantly, it really helped.

Finally, the building was ready and BIMM officially opened. We wanted it to become the best music college in the world. Not the biggest or the most prolific, but the best; the Lamborghini of music colleges if you like. And for a short amount of time we achieved that. Up until Year Three I don't think anyone could compete with what we were delivering in terms of the systems we had and our education style. We didn't have loads of teachers but the teachers we did have were world class and most importantly, they cared, they were there for the right reasons. By 2004 we had 500 students, which was 200 more than we said we'd take. But for those first three years, I was on top of the world. I knew every student by name and everything about their music and their goals. We'd hit the sweet spot of having enough students to provide the income we needed to make BIMM great, but not so many that we couldn't look after them properly.

But then things started getting out of hand. The problem is, when something's good everyone wants to be a part of it. We had 25 Top 40 hits in the first three years. We had musicians touring with massive artists. We kept expanding due to the huge amount of students wanting to come to BIMM and this expansion came with a lot of other implications, such as building size and funding. BIMM was no longer a punky, new, exciting school where you could break the rules, it had become a powerhouse and there was pressure from everywhere telling us what we could and couldn't do. By 2008 I no longer knew all of the students' names – it was impossible, there were 1,500 of them and we'd just opened up a second BIMM centre in Bristol. My life was changing rapidly and I felt that I hadn't done what I'd set out to achieve. Basically, I wanted those first three years for the rest of my life. I wanted to know and help every student. World class education relies on one-to-one interaction like this. I hated that BIMM had become this big, lumbering corporate machine. I was making more money than I'd ever dreamed of but I've never been money oriented. I felt like a fraud and I started to rebel. I shouldn't have. I was never going to win, rebelling against the education establishment. To be brutally honest, I ended up being a bit of an egotistical brat. I started falling out with the other directors and I was seen as a loose cannon because the things I was doing in Years One, Two and Three just weren't working in Year Seven. If you take a student out for a cup of tea in Year One, it's seen as a great level of service. In Year Seven, when it's no longer possible to do this with every student, it's seen as favouritism. The one-to-one time that I so valued with the students was now seen as destructive as opposed to constructive.

In 2009, I decided to sell my share of the company and leave. I remember driving home that day thinking that's it, it's over, it's finished. I was thirty years old. Just like when I was sixteen and failed my GCSEs and nineteen and lost my record deal, I found myself faced with the question: *what am I going to do with the rest of my life?* Even though other people might not see me selling my share in a very successful business as a failure, as far as I was concerned it was unfinished business. I hadn't achieved what I'd set out to do. I would no longer get to build the business further and work with the students. But the good thing about all of the setbacks I'd experienced was that they'd taught me to not to buy into the so-called rule that failure means defeat. As I drove home I briefly considered the idea of retiring. By the time I got home that option was no longer on the table. I went upstairs and into a room we'd been using to store stuff in. I turned a packing box upside down so I had something to write on, grabbed a notepad and pen and wrote at the top of the page: WHAT AM I GOING TO DO WITH THE REST OF MY LIFE?

In the hour since I'd left BIMM I'd gone from a multi-million pound business to a notepad and pen and an upturned box. The first thing I realised was that I wanted to keep learning. I didn't want this to be the end of my story. I wanted it to be the beginning and I had to go back to what I knew and loved best – playing my guitar. My precious 1977 Fender Precision bass had been the one constant in my life, it was the one thing that wouldn't leave me or let me down. I needed to play music again, so I decided to put all of the knowledge I'd gleaned about the music industry into practise by starting a management agency. I knew I'd be able to help bands find work and make money. I decided to start by forming a band so I'd have someone to manage and to make money for the agency and then I'd be able to take on other bands. DK Management has now grown to be one of the largest musical management agencies in the UK. I love helping young musicians make money and strategize their careers.

About two years ago it became clear to me that social media was changing the music industry at lightning speed. For the first time since I got dropped by Parlophone I felt unsure of how the industry worked and I realised that if I was going to stay ahead of the game I'd need to figure it out fast. As I set about finding out all I could about how to use social media as a business and marketing tool for musicians I realised two things:

1. Even though social media is a relatively new thing, people are already being held back by blindly following certain rules
2. The lessons I learned about breaking these rules don't just apply to the music industry – anyone and any business can benefit from what I've learned

So that's how this book came to be. Inside these pages you'll find all of the tricks and tips I've learned in all my years in business because essentially, social media is today's vehicle for business and everything that entails, such as marketing, advertising, insights, customer service, sales and promotion.

There's been a lot of trial and error on my part, which this book will hopefully save you from. And as well as quality advice and inspirational examples, this book also contains a 30 Day Challenge, to help you put all you've learned into action. I guarantee that if you accept the challenge and carry out the daily tasks I set, you will start seeing real results in your business – whatever that might be. But before we get stuck into the world of social media, I want to take a broader look at why it's so important to challenge the rules...

PART ONE

CREATION

CHAPTER ONE

BREAKING THE SCHOOL RULES

'You don't learn to walk by following rules. You learn by doing, and by falling over.'
Richard Branson

First things first, a lot of rules are there for very good reason, a lot of rules are there to keep us safe. If you see a sign telling you not to do something – like drive the wrong way up a one-way street or take a swig from a bottle of bleach – it's because someone's done it before and let's just say, it didn't turn out too well. But the rules I'm interested in talking about here are the rules that shouldn't be there in the first place; rules that if you break them, you won't get hurt, in fact the opposite is true. If you break these so-called rules you could end up achieving things beyond your wildest expectations.

School rules

We first start learning these so-called rules in school. Rules about time-keeping and attendance and appearance and what is meant by success and failure. But these are rules that were established a long, long time ago, to fit the needs of a very different world. The first schools in the UK were set up during the Middle Ages to teach Latin to the aristocracy, to prepare them for entry into the clergy. Back then the Bible and other Christian teachings were written in Latin and the education system was very much tied to the church. Things changed in the nineteenth century with the arrival of the Industrial Revolution, when education became widely available and then compulsory for all children, not just the sons of the rich. Instead of focusing on Latin for religious reasons, schools began focusing on teaching the three R's – reading, writing and arithmetic (and yes, even I know that that's actually one R, a W and an A!). In 1837 an America guy called Horace Mann became Secretary of the Board of Education in Massachusetts. He argued that as well as teaching the three R's, it was just as important that schools taught obedience to authority, regular and prompt attendance and organising time according to a bell ringing, to prepare children for the workplace. Similar changes were introduced in the UK in 1870, with the Forster Education Act making school compulsory for all children aged 5 – 10. So back then, school wasn't about training free-thinking individuals for their own unique brand of success, it was all about training an army of workers who would obey the rules of the workplace.

The trouble with our education system today is that the rules it instils in us haven't really changed in 150 years but everything outside of school has – drastically. We're no longer living in the industrial age. After the arrival of the internet we're living in what I call the creative age, with the imminent arrival of AI and automation set to decimate traditional industries. To thrive in this new era we need to be able to break the rules and think outside of the box. Students need to be inspired not programmed. Classes need to be smaller and tailored to meet the individual kid's strengths and needs but our education system isn't adapting accordingly. OK, so music lessons might now feature Coldplay instead of The Beatles and curriculums might have been broadened to include subjects like Photography and Business Studies but to me, this is just plastering over the cracks. My 14-year-old son is passionate about business and he'd really been looking forward to his Business Studies course. But he came home from his second lesson really disappointed because his teacher had sat at the back marking for the entire period while they watched a video. It's not the teacher's fault – he's a PE teacher who's been drafted in to tick the Business Studies box. Why don't schools bring in experts from outside to teach subjects like these? I'd love to be involved teaching business in a school, to be some kind of business patron.

My biggest bugbear about today's schools are the limited choices. I'm outraged that in 2018 a set curriculum is being forced on children. My son was only allowed to choose four out of his twelve courses. Just think about that for a minute, eight subjects are literally forced upon you. Instead of asking each student, *'where do you excel and what can we nurture in you?'* kids are forced to take subjects they might have no interest in. Why can't they be free to choose the subjects that mean the most to them?

I understand that there can't be total anarchy but ultimately education should be about what's best for the world and evolution and the individual but we're still being taught to conform. We're still being forced to do certain subjects like science, religious studies and maths, even if we're really bad at them or we'll never need them out in the real world. I can't wait for the day I encounter a Roman gladiator walking along Brighton seafront and I'm finally able to put my Latin to use!

What happened to me in school is a great example of how education is letting a hell of a lot of people down and why we need to start questioning the rules. As I said in the Introduction, I failed my GCSEs twice, but this was just a culmination of years of so-called failure in the school system. When I was in junior school part of our regular routine was something called 'fortnightly orders'. Every two weeks the whole class would have to stand and then the teacher would read out our names according to the results we'd got in our work. The highest performing kid got to sit down first. The lowest performing kid would be left standing until last, with all eyes on him or her. I was always the last kid standing, apart from a couple of times when an Iraqi classmate beat me to last place. But he couldn't even speak English so it didn't really count. Week in, week out, the lesson I was being taught by school was that I was the thickest kid in my class, twenty-second out of twenty-two – in every subject. It was really harsh and it really hurt. They also wrote the results in a chart on the wall, so I'd see my name at the bottom every single day.

The so-called rules tell us that with a track record like mine, I was destined for a life-time of dead-end jobs because the education system had filed me in the failure box. But what if it was actually the other way round? **What if it was the education system that failed me?** What if one of my teachers had spotted the potential in me? What if they'd realised that I needed another way of learning to help me thrive? I'm not blaming the teachers. They're bound by a rigid curriculum dictated to them by the government, they're not allowed to challenge the system either. But I can't help thinking things could have been so much better for me in school if I'd been treated differently. Thankfully, I didn't let what happened at school define or defeat me. I remained determined to achieve my goal of doing what I loved in a career in the music industry and I was lucky enough to meet some really inspirational people who helped me enormously.

I liken this kind of thinking to driving to a destination. What if you wanted to go to Manchester and discovered that the M6 was shut? Would you say to yourself, *ah well, looks like I'll never go to Manchester then*, and return back home? Or would you re-programme your sat nav to find an alternative route? Just because one thing doesn't work out, it doesn't mean you should abandon all hope of reaching your goal. You just have to work out another way to get there. So, if you fail your GCSEs, you take a BTEC or get some work experience or teach yourself whatever it is you want to learn. You need to challenge the so-called rules around success and failure. And don't let yourself be pigeon-holed by any false lessons you've been taught about yourself.

Dropping out to leap in

One person who definitely hasn't been pigeon-holed by his experience in school is Sir Richard Branson. A dyslexic, Branson always struggled academically and dropped out of school at the age of sixteen, when he set up his first business running a student magazine. He's now one of the most successful businessmen on the planet. In March 2017, Forbes listed his wealth at an estimated £5 billion.

Another inspirational example of someone who left his academic studies to set up in business is Elon Musk. Despite being so badly bullied in school that he once ended up in hospital, Musk continued his studies to university. But, just two days into his PhD course, he left, deciding to take a chance on the dot-com boom that was just beginning. He never returned to university and went on to become a business magnate, investor, engineer and inventor.

Bill Gates dropped out of Harvard in his junior year to form Micro Soft (which went on to become Microsoft, one of the world's largest tech companies) with his friend Paul Allen. At the age of eleven Elton John received a piano scholarship to go to London's prestigious Royal Academy of Music. But he quit after five years, bored of classical music and bitten by the rock 'n' roll bug, to become a weekend pianist in a local pub. At the age of seventeen he formed a band called Bluesology and by the mid-sixties they were touring with the Isley Brothers. In 1970 he released his first album, *Elton John*, and the first single from it *Your Song* entered the US top ten. The rest is history. David Karp dropped out of an elite school in New York at the age of 15 to develop the microblogging social network Tumblr in the back bedroom of his mum's apartment. He sold it to Yahoo for $1.1 billion in 2013. Film director, Quentin Tarantino also dropped out of school at 15, when he went to work as an usher in a movie theatre and study drama. He's now the winner of two academy awards and has been nominated for several more.

These guys all dropped out of education at some point – **but they dropped out to leap into their dreams and build a life around their passions**. They're great examples of people who haven't played by the rules when it comes to school and have achieved huge success. Disclaimer: I'm not suggesting that everyone drops out of school or saying that people can't do well with a traditional education but I am saying that today's education system is quite one dimensional and doesn't fit everybody. If you don't fit and aren't benefitting from it then staying in the system and racking up crazy amounts of debt is more of a risk than dropping out and gaining experience earlier.

But the rules we learn in school aren't the only ones that need challenging. The world of work is full of them too...

CHAPTER TWO

BREAKING THE WORK RULES

'Your art is what you do when no-one else can tell you how to do it. Your art is the act of taking personal responsibility, challenging the status quo. Changing people.'

Seth Godin, The Linchpin

In his brilliant book, *The Linchpin*, Seth Godin talks about the difference between a job and your art. A job is something you're told to do and something another person could do, making you completely dispensable. My three-hour career in the shampoo factory is a great example of this. I was one of four people who stood around the conveyor belt. One guy picked the bottles out of the box and placed them on the belt. I wiped the tops clean. Another guy then put the bottles back in the box. When I told my supervisor that I thought it might be more effective if one of us did this entire process by lifting the bottles out of the box to clean the tops he told me that 'my job wasn't to think'. I'd been trying to be helpful and save them time and money but initiative wasn't wanted or encouraged. Unlike jobs, your art, according to Godin, is something that's unique to you, and therefore makes you indispensable. It's this art that I believe is essential for success in this new creative age. I'm passionate about helping people find their art (and I class business as art because it's such a creative process; you're building something from nothing). I'm passionate about helping people find the work that makes them a linchpin rather than a cog – and using social media to maximise their chances of success. A vital first step in this process is challenging the so-called rules that exist around the world of work. Here are the rules that I think need to be broken in order to thrive in this new age.

RULE #1: YOU NEED TO WORK IN A SET PLACE AT SET TIMES

The most obvious so-called rules when it comes to employment are when and where you should work. A lot of people and companies are still operating under the false belief that you should work from nine to five in an official workspace. But in the creative age, these so-called rules need to be challenged otherwise there's a danger of them becoming straitjackets. I'm aware that I'm very fortunate because I'm self-employed so I'm in a position to be able create my own rules. But that's exactly why I've written this book – because I want other people to have this kind of life too. This is the great thing about the creative age. We're able to build a career doing the things we love and on our own terms. I don't have any problem with work-life balance because I don't really see my job as work because I enjoy it so much. I work in a very different way to most people. I have certain things I want to get done but I have a lot of flexibility around how and when they get done. For example, I have no problem starting at midday and working until two in the morning. Don't get me wrong, I work very hard to create this kind of freedom for myself. Some days it's insane and I'm shattered. But other days I'm free to do whatever I want to do and when. I'm not on a clock. I know I'll always get stuff done because I won't cut off at 5.30 on the dot. Sometimes, when I can't sleep, I get up and work in the middle of the night, jotting down ideas and checking in on my social media. I actually like working in the middle of the night but I'm not saying this is for everyone. You need to work at the times that suit you the best.

When I employ a new person in my team I'd rather buy them an i-phone or i-pad than a PC because I don't want them to be limited location-wise by a computer. I want them to be able to work anywhere. I want them to be excited at the possibilities this presents. As long they hit the targets they're set I don't really care where they work. I think most, if not all of us probably work best like this. I know that if I was made to sit in a cubicle all day, every day I wouldn't be very efficient. I'd feel trapped and frustrated. Internet and mobile phone technology has revolutionised the way we work. We should embrace the freedom it gives us rather than resist it. It's OK to rebel against this crap – seriously.

RULE #2: YOU NEED TO GET A 'PROPER JOB'

Another unwritten rule that exists around work is that you need to get a 'proper job'. This is a hangover from how things used to be and definitely needs to be challenged. The trouble is, people are triggered when you do something outside of the norm. Chances are, if you pluck up the courage to follow your dream, you'll hit some kind of resistance from family and friends. I once received an email from a sixteen-year-old kid. He told me that he wanted to be a musician but his parents were both doctors and wanted him to follow them down the medical path. To them, being a doctor was a proper job and equalled success. I told him that he had to talk to them because if he became a doctor and hated it every single day that wouldn't be a success at all, it would be a massive failure. Surely happiness trumps money when it comes to success? As a parent I do get it. I understand that we're more fearful of our kids failing than they are and therefore we try to steer them down certain paths in life for our own sanity. But the reality is, if we force them to do something they hate they will have failed. For me, it's about communication; asking my son what he really wants to do and why. And as long as it isn't something dodgy like being a drug dealer – or a letting agent – I'll respect his wishes because I know that ultimately he'll be so much happier being able to choose his own path in life.

RULE #3: INDUSTRY-SPECIFIC RULES

Every industry comes with its own set of so-called rules that need to be challenged and the music industry is a great example of this. Here are just some of the so-called rules that no longer apply in the music business yet many people are still blindly following:

- An album should have twelve songs
- A song should be three minutes
- A presentation / gig / event should be in a venue
- You need to have a record deal
- An advert needs to be thirty seconds

••••

This last one about advertising applies to any industry and seriously needs to be challenged. It's a rule that comes from the world of TV. But television adverts had their heyday back in the 1960s before the internet, when they were one of the best ways for people to find out about things such as holidays, products, or services. The commercial break was part of the television experience. But now they're seen as an annoyance, something to skip, a reason to go and put the kettle on. We can get all the info we need online, the last thing we want is a hard sell interrupting our viewing. With the advent of social media, the rules around advertising have changed and it's the people who think outside the box who are gaining. There will be a *lot* more on this subject later in this book. But for now, are there any rules in your industry that you're blindly following? How could you break them in order to achieve greater success?

RULE #4: IF YOU FAIL IN BUSINESS YOU SHOULD GIVE UP

I've started several companies that have failed but I don't think of it as failing, I think of it as all part of the journey. Let me give you an example...

One time, I was trying to get a PR company involved in a business I owned. I tried every local PR company I could find. I was willing to pay whatever their going rate was for their services. But I had no joy. Some said no because it wasn't their specialist field and some had a conflict of interest but most of them didn't get back to me. I realised that they must be letting other people down like this. So I thought, *sod it, I'm going to start my own PR company*. What can I say, I'm a pretty impulsive person. I spent six months building a PR company and hiring a team. I got an office and created a website ... and then realised that I didn't know anything about how to do PR. I didn't have the experience to make it work. I realised I was at a crossroads. I could either change the business model and bring in more experienced people at a lot more cost, or I could change what I wanted to do. The whole thing had been a knee-jerk reaction and I found it relatively easy to accept that it didn't work and move on. The lesson I learned was that you need to know when to accept that something isn't working for you and pick a different route. I didn't see it as a failure at all. Just as I wouldn't see a journey as a failure if I decided to pick a new route. When it comes to business, I'm a firm believer that if you focus on enjoying the journey and all its ups and downs you can't fail. As fighter Conor McGregor says: 'I never fail. I either win or learn.'

RULE #5: THERE ISN'T THE TIME TO PURSUE YOUR DREAM CAREER

This is one that comes up a lot but personally I think it's bullshit. If you want something badly enough you will make the time. For the first six months I was setting up BIMM I was working from nine until six. Then I'd drive for an hour and a half to Brighton for meetings until midnight or one in the morning and then I'd drive the hour and a half back and get up and go to work the next morning. If I hadn't found the time in those early days I never would have been part of what would become one of the biggest music schools in the world.

A few years ago a French kid came for a tutorial with me. He was music production student and he told me that he'd been asked to do an internship at AIR studios. AIR are world famous, state of the art studios founded by George Martin. This was a massive opportunity but the kid was unsure whether to do it. 'They want me to do the graveyard shift,' he told me. 'And I have to study and work because it's unpaid and I don't know how to fit it in. I won't have time to sleep.'

I told him in no uncertain terms that he had to do whatever it took to make it work. 'Even if you have to sleep on someone's floor. Even if it nearly kills you, don't fuck this up. It's too important.'

Two months later, I went to see a film at the local cinema and the French guy was the usher who showed me to my seat. When he recognised me he looked really sheepish. I said, 'You didn't take the studio gig, did you?' He shook his head. I couldn't believe it. Faced with the biggest opportunity of his life he told himself that he didn't have the time. Yes, it would have been painful and would have involved sacrifice but if he'd done it the rewards could have been huge.

RULE #6: YOU SHOULD ALWAYS TAKE NO FOR AN ANSWER

A great example of someone who used work experience as a launch-pad for a hugely successful career was our old head of song-writing at BIMM. He started his career back when he was a teenager by phoning up a studio and asking for work experience. They agreed to let him do two weeks. When the two weeks were over he continued turning up anyway. At first, the people at the studio were a little bemused but he was so keen to work and so good at what he did they let him carry on – and on and on. Then one day he found a paying job, so he didn't show up. He'd made himself so indispensable by this point that the studio immediately offered to match the salary. He went on to be the engineer on some of the best-selling albums of the 80s and 90s.

When I employ staff I'm looking for people like him. People who Seth Godin calls linchpins. I'm looking for someone who's prepared to think instead of just do. I'm looking for someone who'll challenge me. My Social Media Architect (I like breaking the rules when it comes to job titles too) Sara is a great example of this. She got in touch with me via Twitter asking if I offered any internships. I said no but she persuaded me to make an exception. She was living in France at the time but she said she'd pay for herself to come over. I was really impressed by her enthusiasm and initiative. Three months later I offered her a permanent, paid job. She's been with us for over a year now and she's in charge of all of my video content. I offered her the job because I want to work with people have the balls to make sacrifices and work hard for what they want to achieve, people who don't automatically take no for an answer.

RULE #7: SOCIAL MEDIA IS JUST A DEPARTMENT

And now we come to the crux of this book: **social media is no longer just a department of your business, it *is* your business.** All the old departments: HR, customer service, marketing, advertising, sales and PR, now come under the umbrella of social media. The old rule when it came to social media was that it was just an advertising tool – but it's so much more powerful than that. When you know how, social media also allows you to provide all of the following:

- greater understanding of your demographic
- building relationships
- excellent customer service
- branding through storytelling
- being seen as an authority
- free virality

I can remember the moment when it all clicked into place and hit me like a freight train that it's all about social media. It was a couple of years ago and I was working as a consultant for ACM, helping with their marketing and sales. I was sitting in the office thinking, *hang on a minute, customer service is now all about social media, marketing is all about social media, sales and HR are all about social media — it's all about social media, and I don't know nearly enough about it!* I realised that this was a major problem because I like building businesses, but the rules hadn't just changed — they'd completely gone. There's a common misconception that social media is advertising but it's not. Social media is what people are doing and consuming and, as marketers, creatives and entrepreneurs, it's our job to get in front of them while they're doing it. That day it hit me I realised I had two choices. I could either very quickly learn all there was to learn about social media or I was going to be forced out of the game and made extinct by tomorrow's entrepreneurs. So I decided to learn. Full disclosure, I have a very obsessive personality. As soon as I started learning about social media the obsession kicked in and it was 24/7. I wasn't just learning about it, I was *in* it. From watching videos, to having meetings, to experimenting with all the different platforms. Because I already had twenty years' experience in business, marketing and sales, plus my obsessive nature, I got good at it very quickly. It was the equivalent of me learning to ride a motorbike after years of driving a car. All the controls were in different places but I knew the rules of the road so I was able to learn faster than someone who'd never driven before.

Of course, in this rapidly changing world, things could all have changed again in five years' time but for now, social media is the vehicle. It's where TV and radio and magazine advertising used to be, and door-to-door salesmen before them. Social media is now where all the attention is. And if we want to succeed and become indispensable in our work, whatever that might be, we need to be there too. What I've learned has really excited me. Technology and social media have revolutionised everything. The creative age has arrived and the old rules have gone and even better, we now have complete control. There's no gatekeeper any more, the internet is the middle man. In this new era it's creativity that's going to win on every level and it's social media that's going to allow us to do so. Let me show you why...

CHAPTER THREE

FINDING THE G-SPOT

'*The only way to do great work is to love
what you do.*'

Steve Jobs

The fact that you're reading a book with 'rule breakers' in the title implies that you want to build a career on your own terms. You want to get paid for doing what you love. The great news is, social media can really help you achieve this – if you know how to use it effectively.

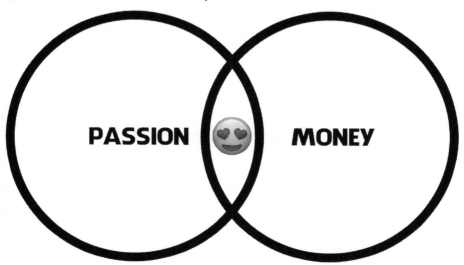

On the left-hand side of the ven diagram above we have PASSION. This is where you do whatever the hell you want to, experimenting and learning and having fun with your passion, whatever that might be.

MONEY

On the right-hand side we have MONEY. These are the things we do to earn a living. Things that we may not feel passionately about but do out of necessity; the bar work you do to subsidise your fledgling coaching practise, the mundane office job you do to finance your side-hustle selling home-made greetings cards.

THE SWEET SPOT

The small overlap between the two is the sweet spot, the money shot, what we're all striving for. This is where you're able to do exactly what you want to do *and* get paid for it. The trouble with this overlap is that it's almost impossible to find. We're talking unicorn here. We're talking g-spot. So often when we try to get paid for doing exactly what we want to, we hit a roadblock.

This book is a perfect example. Before I started work on it I got approached out of the blue by a publishing company. They told me that they loved what I was doing and said they wanted to sign me up and publish a book by me. I was gobsmacked. The last book I'd read was *Fantastic Mr Fox*, it had never occurred to me that someone might want to publish a book by me. And they were offering to pay me money before I'd even written a word. Sold! So I went for a meeting with the publisher and in the first five minutes he asked me if I had an idea for a title.

'I'd like it to be called *Fuck Plan B*,' I said.

He looked really shocked. 'Do you mean f*** with asterix?' he asked.

'No,' I replied. 'Fuck with all the letters.'

'I'm afraid that's impossible,' he told me.

'What do you mean it's impossible? Surely I should be allowed to choose the title for my own book.'

But the publisher wouldn't budge. It instantly took me back to being a kid dealing with record labels and I got a sinking feeling. It was just like being told what can and can't be on your album cover. I realised that if I signed a book deal I'd be signing away my soul. The creativity would be sucked out of it because other people would be in control. And I couldn't do that with this book because the whole point of this book is about being in full control of your career and creations and doing things your own unique way. So I thought, *fuck this I don't need your book deal, I'll build an audience and market it myself.* When it comes to this book, I'm firmly in the PASSION section of the ven diagram. I passionately believe that this book needs to be made, that its message needs to be told and I'm not going to sell out. Now, I know what you're thinking – *this book isn't called Fuck Plan B, it's called The Rule-Breaker's Guide to Social Media.* But that's because once I got focused on exactly what it was that I wanted to write and how I could help people the most, I realised that it was all about breaking the rules and social media. The original title wouldn't have matched the content, it wouldn't have made any sense. If I was driven purely by money I'd have said to the publisher, 'OK, you tell me what to do and I'll put something down and you can re-write it however you want to.' But if I make any money from this book I want to make it from the sweet spot in the middle of the diagram because then I won't have sacrificed my passion.

Reaching that sweet spot involves a lot of hard work and compromise. The compromise comes in the form of marketing and audience-building. You can't just say: 'I created this business / service / product, why isn't anyone buying it?' The sweet spot means that if you're doing all of the creation on your own terms, you have to do all of the marketing and distribution yourself too. If you're saying, 'To hell with generic fashion, I want to make clothes for people who love 1950s rockabilly style', you have to find these people. If you're saying, 'Fuck pop music, I want to make sixty minute prog rock songs,' you have to seek out the people who want sixty minute prog rock songs. This involves crazy hard work on the marketing side. Hours and hours every single day on your social media accounts … for maybe five to ten years. And I don't mean advertising here, I mean audience-building. If you want to get paid for doing what you love you can't get away with doing the bare minimum, like a couple of Facebook posts and a one-off YouTube video. I see so many people doing this and I just don't get it. Why put so much time and effort into creating something and then only spend a few weeks marketing it? If you want people to buy into your passion you have to find them and build a community. Look after this community like they've never been looked after before. Bring value to them every single day until you reach a point where you can begin to monetise your passion. You can't do it immediately. You have to wait until they're in love with what you do and really value it. Then and only then you can expect to make money from your passion.

The truth about numbers

Some social media experts argue that numbers aren't the be all and end all but come on, if you're serious about using social media to promote your brand or message, numbers are bound to be important to you. The fact is, numbers bring credibility. If you're chatting to someone in the pub and you find out that they have 50,000 followers on Instagram, chances are you're going to be pretty impressed. Whether we like it or not, big numbers open doors. Most people don't know how to get big numbers on their platforms, so achieving tens of thousands of followers is seen as some kind of Holy Grail. But there are *two* key aspects to numbers that we need to pay attention to when it comes to social media:

1. Getting the audience
2. What you do with the audience

Having number 1 without number 2 is pointless, unless you're just showing off. If you're using social media for your business you need to be able to convert your audience's attention into money. It's as simple as that. Otherwise, what you're doing is just a hobby. Say you're a hairdresser and you get featured on morning TV. Suddenly you gain 500 followers on Twitter. Brilliant. But if none of those people pay attention to your posts or spend money on your products or services then those numbers are just an ego metric. As social media marketers and business people, it's vital we realise that it's not just about getting the numbers on social media, it's what we do with those numbers that really counts – and that's where this book is really going to help you.

It might take years of hours a day hard graft but if you're prepared to do it then the great news is, the g-spot is actually findable! So, get clear on where you are. If you're motivated by money that's fine, find ways to earn money. And if you don't need to make money from your passion, that's fine too. But if you want to be paid for doing what you love, you need to seriously up your social media marketing game. Let's get stuck in…

CHAPTER FOUR

YOUTUBE

'Our goal is to have YouTube on every screen —
to take it from the PC to the living room and the
mobile phone.

Steve Chen, co-founder of YouTube

Of all the social media platforms available, YouTube is the one that gives the most value for me personally, but it's all relative. YouTube gives me value because I produce a lot of different kinds of video content, from educational talks, to Q&A shows, to vlogs, but it can be a difficult platform for people to crack as it's harder to boost your content on YouTube than somewhere like Facebook. I liken having a YouTube channel to having your own television station. Stop and think about that for a moment, let the reality sink in. **YouTube gives you the freedom to share as much video content as you want, when you want. For free!** Through the playlist feature it enables you to create separate channels within your channel, a bit like BBC i-player. So you can create playlists for as many different categories as you like: daily vlogs, Q&As, comedy sketches, documentaries, promo and music videos, even feature length films. Whatever you want to create, whenever you want to put it out there, it's entirely up to you. You are the controller of your channel, in charge of scheduling and programming and organising your content however you want and the possibilities that provides you with are endless. But already a set of so-called rules has sprung up around YouTube, threatening to hamper our creativity. Let's take a look at them and why they make no sense, before moving on to see how you can use YouTube to grow your business or creative venture to the full.

THE YOUTUBE RULES ... AND WHY YOU SHOULD BREAK THEM

RULE #1: Your videos need to be polished to perfection

It's so important not to be intimidated by the highly polished videos on YouTube as this actually means there's a gap in the market for you. Let me explain why...

When Bruce and I left ACM to set up BIMM, ACM was at the most powerful it had ever been. As I mentioned earlier, they were doing so well they'd just invested £2 million in creating a state of the art building. It looked like a spaceship and was seriously impressive. Each sector of the building was a different colour. Even the toilet seats were colour-coded and sparkled with glitter. It was designed to make such a powerful first impression to any prospective student they'd find it hard to say no. For a musician it was like being a kid in a sweetshop, there were guitars everywhere. In YouTube terms ACM was the equivalent of the expertly shot vlog, with full studio lighting, set and make-up. We left when it was at the top and set up BIMM with next to nothing. As I said before, in YouTube terms we were like the kid in the poorly lit bedroom vlogging on their phone. But actually the fact that we were so unpolished worked massively in our favour. In those early days BIMM seemed way more rock 'n' roll than the polished ACM. Musicians liked us because we were fresh and raw and real. And the same was true of our premises. Entering BIMM was like entering a guitar museum. You'd never find the wrong guitar or amp there. There was a reason for everything. We were really picky. We bought second-hand because we knew that an amp from the 1960s with a great backstory would mean more to people than something brand new. For example, being able to say to people, 'this is exactly the kind of amp Angus Young used when ACDC recorded *Back in Black*,' really meant something. We prided ourselves on being gear geeks. The irony is that now BIMM has got massive it's no way near as rock 'n' roll any more. There's definitely an opening for someone to come along and take advantage – someone else who is hungry and raw. And the exact same principle applies to YouTube.

Take a look at the earliest videos made by today's top YouTubers. You'll find that they were unpolished and rough around the edges but it didn't stop them becoming successful. In fact, it was what *made* them successful. People like things that are a little rough around the edges because they feel authentic. **So, every time a YouTuber moves up the ladder and becomes slicker it's not stopping other people from being successful, it's actually creating an opening.** YouTube revolves around creativity and authenticity. When you're starting out, your job isn't to compete with the more polished videos and channels. Your job is to create something fresh and new and exciting that people will want to engage with and share.

A great example of this is Canadian singer Ruth B. One night, after watching an episode of the TV series *Once Upon a Time* featuring the character Peter Pan, she felt inspired to write a song. So she went down to her piano in her pyjamas and came up with a four-line chorus, which she recorded on her phone. She posted the six second video on Vine and went to bed. Within a week the video had got 84,000 likes and loads of comments from people wanting to hear the whole song. She hadn't even written it yet! The video was just of her hand playing a four-line chorus on the piano. There was no studio lighting, no expertly filmed shots. The camera was wobbly and hand-held. She did everything 'wrong' technically but it didn't matter at all. People don't want perfection. They want creativity and authenticity. And in this case, 84,000 people wanted it in one week. Encouraged by the overwhelming response, Ruth B wrote the rest of the song. She recorded it and posted it on YouTube, in an equally rough around the edges video. The video went viral and the song became the smash hit *Lost Boy*.

Author, business coach and host of the YouTube show *Marie TV*, Marie Forleo, is another example of someone who has achieved great success on the platform. The original episodes of her weekly show consisted of her simply talking into the camera on her phone. Now the show is professionally filmed in a studio, reaches viewers in 195 different countries and has had close to 38 million views. Her first videos might have been rough around the edges but they were authentic and genuinely helpful and this is what helped her channel to grow.

The only way you become polished at something is by doing it a lot. It's the famous 10,000 hour rule written about by author and speaker Malcolm Gladwell in his book *Outliers: The Story of Success*. According to Gladwell, it takes 10,000 hours of doing something to become an expert at it. The fact is, we have to put the time and effort in if we want to be great at something and we all have to start at the beginning and learn as we go. It's the only way *to* learn. But if you keep showing up and creating the content, you're going to get better with every video posted.

THE 1% FORMULA FOR SUCCESS

I look at it like this; **if, with every video you make, you get one percent better, then after one hundred videos, you'll be one hundred percent better.** It's about taking one step at a time instead of a huge jump. Whenever I look at one of my pictures or videos I try not to think of them as good or bad, I try and think, *what will my content be like in three or five pictures' time?* So don't get down and think you can't compete. Think of it like the story about the hare and the tortoise. Be patient and keep taking small steps. Be willing to play around and be creative and remember to view your channel like your own TV station. I'm constantly experimenting with the content on my channel with several very different style playlists, from my more polished *Ask Damo Show*, to more heartfelt, handheld vlogs shot in my car.

RULE #2: You should always post at the same time

Why? Seriously, would you ever tell the controller of the BBC that they should only put their programmes out at 3pm on a Thursday? There's an unwritten rule that's sprung up around the best time to post on YouTube to get the most viewers but I don't subscribe to this rule. For a start, everyone's demographic is different. It could be that your target audience loves nothing more than watching YouTube late at night. Also, if the most popular time to post is 8pm, how are you going to be able to cut through the noise? If you stick to the so-called rules you could be missing the peak viewing time for your kind of content or you could be lost in the noise of everyone else posting. Experiment with different times. **Find out which time works best for you and your audience.**

RULE #3: You should only put out a set number of videos per week

I think this rule is complete bullshit. Once again because it all depends on your audience and the quality of your content. If you have different playlists with different themes and you're uploading to each of them in turn then you're not bombarding your audience with the same content over and over again. Experiment to find a level of output that works for you. **One thing I will say is that regularity is key**. The more you create, the better you'll become and you'll build an expectation in your viewers. If you commit to posting every day you should post every day. Otherwise your viewer might become disappointed and go elsewhere. Equally, if you just post once a week that's fine, as long as you post when you say you will. If your viewer likes what you do they'll look out for your content but if they feel they can't rely on you they'll drift off. I know this from my own viewing habits. **There's no such thing as too much content, just shit content**. The website Lad Bible puts out a new piece of content every forty minutes to an hour, that's between fifteen and twenty-five pieces of content a day. It clearly isn't putting people off as, at the time of writing, they have over 30 million likes on Facebook.

RULE #4: The ultimate length is ten minutes.

Not if you're crap on camera it's not. If you're better in short snappy videos just keep them to a minute long. Some people are more engaging over a shorter period of time and that's fine. Joe Wicks became famous for doing fifteen second meal videos on Vine. If he'd started doing fifteen minute videos on YouTube he might not have stood out from the crowd. Don't be afraid to experiment with the length of your videos and pay attention to what your audience likes. Find out how much time they like to spend watching videos. If they're busy people and only watch content in short bursts you should tailor the length of your videos accordingly. Ultimately, when it comes to YouTube **you're trading your content for someone's time and these days, people *really value* their time**. The rise of companies like Uber and Air B'n'B are proof of this. If you're saying to your viewers on YouTube, '*Give me your three minutes of time and I'll show you me jumping out of a plane, naked, eating a hamster*,' they'll probably see it as a fair trade. But if you're saying, '*Give me your sixty minutes of time and I'll show you me reading from the phone directory*,' it probably ain't gonna happen. This highlights how important your titles and thumbnail images are too – they're your bid for your viewer's time. Make them count.

It's great to view the whole time thing in this way, switching it round to your viewer's point of view. Think of your own viewing habits. **What makes you**

ignore a YouTube video, or hit stop after just a few seconds? And what makes you willing to invest your valuable time? I will happily trade ten minutes of my time for a Casey Neistat video because I know I'm really going to enjoy what he has to offer. He brings a lot of value to my ten minutes. Consider this when you're creating your own content and deciding upon the length. But don't blindly follow someone else's rule. What works for them may not work for you.

Following the house rules

Having said all of that about breaking the rules, YouTube do have certain house rules that you need to respect. **YouTube's house rules all revolve around the consumption and wellbeing of the viewer.** All they want is to keep the viewer on their site for as long as possible. They can only achieve this by paying close attention to statistics. If YouTube see that a video is being viewed a lot they try to get it in front of as many other eyes as possible. It's all about getting people to stay on their site *forever* – their ultimate goal is to get you to never leave. YouTube rewards the creators who provide value and keep viewers on there for as long as possible. If your heading is clickbait and people click on it then click straight off again YouTube will make note of this and won't bother sharing it because it won't help keep people on their site. So the key is thinking like YouTube. **How are you going to get people to find you and want to stay?** When people subscribe to your channel it's more of a hard-core commitment than liking your Facebook page. People tend to be a lot more frugal with their YouTube subscriptions, so when they subscribe it's definitely because they want to see more. It's harder to earn a YouTube subscription than an Instagram or Facebook follow but it's well worth the effort. When you have subscribers you can create a real sense of community and they're way more likely to watch and find your content. Think about it from a consumer's point of view. It's a lot harder to scroll back through someone's Facebook page to find something than it is on their YouTube channel. The layout of a YouTube page makes it much easier for a viewer to scan through your content. If they want to go back to your very first video they can find it in seconds. But imagine trying to do that on a Facebook page. Because of this, I first and foremost make social media content that's YouTube friendly and then break it down and repackage it for other platforms. YouTube is my starting point. YouTube is my television channel. Let's look in more detail at how it can help you...

••••

Greater understanding of your demographic

YouTube is a search engine but most people miss that fact. They want to think of it as a library – a place to store their video content. But, **if you understand that most people use YouTube to look for things, you can create content to help them find you.** Think about your own viewing habits for a moment and the kind of things you look for on YouTube. These days it tends to be that if you want to find a business or a service like a plumber you go to Google but if you want to learn something or be entertained you go straight to YouTube. *How to cook an omelette, assemble a bookshelf, write a song, inter-rail across Europe, get a six-pack,* it's all on there. Hopefully your content will fit into the educational or entertainment category – or both. To really succeed on YouTube you need to tweak your videos to fit the fact that it's a search engine and make your channel as visible as possible. And don't forget that YouTube is owned by the biggest search engine in the world, Google. They are very, very good at what they do.

A great example of someone who's embraced the search engine aspect of YouTube is Andy Guitar. His channel has over half a million subscribers and it features the number one most viewed guitar lesson on YouTube. Andy is very good at consistency and posts one or two things per day. He's also very clever with his content. **He thinks about what's searchable first and then he makes the video.** An example of this are his guitar tutorials. When Andy did a guitar tutorial to *Let it Be* by The Beatles it got 26,000 views. When he did one for *Boulevard of Broken Dreams* by Green Day, it got 82,000 views. Then Andy found out that the most searched song on YouTube was *Galway Girl* by Ed Sheeran, so he did a tutorial on that and it got 345,000 views.

Another way in which Andy works the search engine aspect of YouTube is by asking himself what words or phrases his target viewer would search for. When someone has just bought a new guitar and doesn't know how to play it what's the kind of thing they'll put in the search engine? Andy will incorporate that into the title of his video. Here are three examples from his channel. Can you see how they're exactly the kind of thing a viewer might search for?

How to change chord on a guitar
Simple guide to guitar amp controls
How to hold a guitar properly

••••

The titles are so important here because you have to anticipate what the viewers are going to search for. And to get your video to rise up the list you also need to include the title in the first line of your description and the meta tags. You can add all this during the editing process.

Top Ten Tips are another very searchable title. When Andy first recommended I try them I have to admit I cringed – it all felt a bit cheesy to me. But it really worked. The first Top Ten video I did quickly became my most successful video to date and I now have an entire playlist devoted to Top Tens.

Creating engagement

Another thing I thought was really cheesy when I started YouTubing was the call to action. You know the kind of thing: *'Hit the subscribe button!'* *'Let me know in the comments below!'* etc. But it turns out these calls to action are a great way of engaging with your audience because they actually work. If you prompt your viewer to get involved they will. The first time I actually asked people to subscribe to my channel in one of my videos I got a week's worth of subscribers in a couple of hours. People need reminding. It's not necessarily that they won't subscribe, it's just they haven't thought about it. It was a great lesson and I love the interactive element of the YouTube comments. By asking your viewer to comment it's like you're giving them permission to engage. Some key tried and tested formulas for YouTube videos are:

- Shows
- Top Tens
- Vlogs

Shows can be performance or education based, think motivational talk or Q&A. The word show also indicates that it's consistent, ongoing content, which viewers really love. Top Ten videos are great for searchability. If you're trying to get a point across and you wrap it into a top ten the searchability goes through the roof. People seem to really like lists. Vlogs are great because they trigger emotion and people are naturally inquisitive and like to get a more personal take on things. Vlogs can also be highly addictive viewing.

The format that gets the most engagement from my viewers are the vlogs. It's ironic because for a while I was paying people to professionally shoot and edit my vlogs. Then I made one on the spur of the moment on my phone on my own in my car and it got way more interaction. As I said before, people love things that are more informal and real on YouTube and I think that when they see you opening up in an honest way it encourages them to engage.

Another thing I've realised when it comes to audience engagement on You-Tube is that you should show your viewers the rough with the smooth. If you're posting regular vlogs and they're all relentlessly cheery there's a danger your audience will disengage because this isn't real life. Everyone has good days and bad days and sometimes you should share the bad as well as the good. It en-courages a sense of trust with your viewer if you open up and are honest with them. With my content it's not about being inspirational, it's about being the instruction manual. I want to teach people how to do things. If you bought a piece of flat-pack furniture from Ikea and were struggling to put it together you wouldn't appreciate me cheering on from the sidelines, yelling things like 'You're the greatest!' or 'You're awesome, you've totally got this!' Chances are I'd get a piece of flat-pack wrapped round my head. I'm sure you'd prefer some empathy and practical advice.

Excellent customer service

A YouTube channel offers you a great way of providing excellent customer ser-vice. Through the viewer comments and reactions to your videos you're able to find out what people think of you and your content. And, if there are any problems, YouTube gives you a platform to help rectify them. It's amazing how powerful fixing someone's problem – even though it's been created by you in the first place – is when it comes to customer service. If you do it in the right way you can actually make new fans. If you get a complaint on YouTube don't ignore it, deal with it and offer a way of making amends. People will be impressed by the way you take ownership of the problem and care about your viewers. Even if you get mindless criticism from trolls it's an opportunity to show people who you are and what you stand for. If you do something people don't like they will definitely let you know about it on YouTube! **But if you deal with criticism maturely and responsibly, if you own your mistakes and rectify them, anyone observing is bound to be impressed**. I once got some extremely negative com-ments on a video on my channel. They were from someone who used to work for me and got sacked and doesn't like me in the slightest. He went into great detail about what a c*** he thought I was and how he thought I'd single-handedly wrecked the music industry. I'll be honest with you, his comments stung and my first reaction was one of anger. But then I realised that if I reacted negatively I'd just make myself look like a dick – and in public too. So I took a deep breath and posted a reply offering to meet him for a cup of tea and a chat about the issues he had with me. He didn't take me up on my offer but at least I feel like anyone reading the comments will see that I tried to rectify things. When it comes to negative comments of a personal nature you can take the wind out of someone's sails and look like a hero for not getting involved and for doing the right thing.

Branding through storytelling

People always remember a good story. If I was starting a new business and thinking about how I was going to market a new product it would always be through telling stories. In my opinion when it comes to social media, YouTube is the best medium for telling stories. In this regard it's also the most under-utilised social media tool on the market. It seems as if almost every business has a YouTube channel because they feel they ought to but then they sit there not getting used. When I see this it drives me nuts because it's a waste of such a powerful tool.

Vlogs are a great way of branding and marketing through storytelling. They're a great way of letting your audience know the story behind your product, service or brand. One thing I figured out very quickly is that people always want to know your backstory. They want to know where you came from and what you stand for. Most people focus on their story from today, for example in a daily vlog. But just because you know your backstory it doesn't mean your audience does. And even if your oldest viewers do, new people will hopefully be coming across your channel on a regular basis. It definitely helps to make sure that they'll have a way of finding out your backstory if they want to, for example by creating a 'story so far' video. Have you made a video describing your backstory? If not, don't worry, help is at hand later on in this book, in the 30 Day Challenge.

Once you have your backstory covered you need to start thinking in terms of story in pretty much all you create. There's a story in every product and service you offer and it's down to you to tell it in a compelling and original way. **The number one reason storytelling is so important when it comes to brand and marketing is because people remember a good story**. It sinks into their brains way more effectively than a load of boring facts or stats. Tell us the story about why you became a guitarist and how you formed your band. Tell us the story about why you created your latest service. What does it mean to you personally? Who or what first inspired your creation? In a recent vlog on my YouTube channel I told my viewers the story of how I felt I had failed at BIMM. I told them the story to help them try and reframe the way they look at failure in their own lives. It got a ton of positive engagement in the comments. Storytelling also helps you to build trust.

Being seen as an authority

This is where YouTube is hands down the best platform because of its search engine capability and the way people consume its content. People consume other social media in a more distracted way and usually with no sound. We flick through our Facebook while we're making a cup of tea or doing other things. But with YouTube, the consumer is way more focused; they watch the content like they're watching a film. Because of this you can create a lot more intense, educational marketing for your YouTube channel. My top ten tips videos are basically tutorials. I also have a playlist for the lectures I've given. Your YouTube content doesn't have to be educational but if you don't utilise this aspect of the platform you're missing a trick. Another great thing about YouTube is that, **because of its search engine facility, your content is there to be found forever**. No-one's going to bother scrolling back through three months' worth of your Facebook videos but they can easily find them on YouTube.

What educational content could you offer your viewers? What are the frequently asked questions of your customers, the kind of questions they'd put in a search engine, that you are qualified to answer? By creating videos that help your target audience in this way, you're creating content that is searchable and ever-green – and shareable too.

Going viral

Going viral on YouTube is a powerful thing, the trouble is, you don't get to decide what goes viral – everyone else does. But there are definitely things you can do to try and increase the odds of it happening. Consistency and momentum are key. Keep showing up. Keep experimenting and trying different things. Remember that your content doesn't have to be polished and perfect to go viral. I'm a big fan of entrepreneur and internet personality Gary Vaynerchuck. One of his first viral YouTube videos was of him in the dark, on a plane, having a rant into the camera on his phone. The lighting is terrible and it clearly wasn't scripted but it did brilliantly. Check it out. It's called 'A *rant from the heart, hip and head.*' As with the Ruth B viral video, everything about it from a polished production point of view was wrong. But what was right was that it was very real and it gained him one hundred thousand more subscribers for his channel.

Another great example of a something going viral on YouTube is the video Casey Neistat made about bike lanes in New York City. He was inspired to make it after a cop gave him a ticket and fined him fifty dollars for not riding in the bike lane. In the three minute video Neistat cycles around the bike lanes of New York sticking rigidly to the law and crashing into all of the obstacles he encounters, including construction works, a delivery truck, a cab – and a police car! The point he was making was that surely the police should fine the people blocking the bike lanes, not the cyclists for swerving out of the way to avoid a collision. His video went viral within twenty-four hours and attracted mainstream media attention because it was creative, entertaining and authentic – Neistat genuinely crashed into everything he encountered, keeping it very real – and it tapped into something lots of people felt passionately about. And because they felt so passionately about it they shared it.

Think about the videos you've shared with your friends. What was it about them that made you want to share them? Making content that deeply moves people will also move them to share it with others.

REAL + PASSION + CREATIVITY

Use these three words as a checklist before you create any new content for your channel.

YOUTUBE RECAP

- YouTube is like having your own TV channel. It gives you the freedom to share as much content as you want, when you want. For free!
- Every time a YouTuber moves up the ladder and becomes slicker it's not stopping other people from being successful, it's actually creating an opening.

- If, with every video, you get one percent better, then after one hundred videos, you'll be one hundred percent better.
- Find out which time works best for you and your audience.
- Regularity is key.
- You're trading your content for someone's time and these days, people *really value* their time.
- YouTube's house rules all revolve around the consumption and wellbeing of the viewer.
- Think about what's searchable first and then make the video.
- If you deal with criticism maturely and responsibly anyone observing is bound to be impressed.
- The reason that storytelling is so important when it comes to marketing and brand is because people remember a good story.
- YouTube's search engine facility means that your content is there to be found forever.

CHAPTER FIVE

FACEBOOK THE MONSTER

'Facebook was not built originally to be a company. It was built to accomplish a social mission – to make the world more open and connected.'

Mark Zuckerberg

YouTube might be the best social media platform for storytelling but when it comes to overall platform capabilities, it's pretty one dimensional in comparison to Facebook. In social media marketing terms, Facebook is an absolute monster. **It's an unstoppable force because the possibilities it offers are endless**. It's like YouTube is the set menu in a restaurant and Facebook is the *'all you can eat'* buffet. And yet I see so many business owners, creatives and entrepreneurs failing to utilise it effectively.

A quick word about algorithms...

A huge concern people have when it comes to social media marketing are algorithms. Facebook has updated its algorithm regularly over the last ten years but in 2018 it changed it more drastically than ever before, in order to cut down on marketing messages. Within the space of a week my Facebook reach dropped to 10-20% of what it was before. This drastic change sent many business people and marketers into a tailspin but I think it's a great development. People had been complaining about the amount of 'noise' on Facebook for years and as marketers, it was so hard to cut through. Effectively, Facebook is now a pay to play arena when it comes to marketing, just as print and media advertising always has been. Of course, we don't know how long it will be before it changes again but for now this is the state of play.

Because people had got used to having it for free many of them have thrown their toys out of the pram and have stopped marketing on Facebook. But this means that it's now far easier for those of us who are prepared to pay to get our message heard. We had it far too good on Facebook for far too long. You wouldn't expect to get free advertising in a newspaper or a magazine or on TV. The fact that you get any free reach at all on Facebook is brilliant. The change in the algorithm means that people will now make less marketing content at a higher level because there's no point in just churning things out. Now it comes down to who actually knows their stuff and I love that. This is the time to double down and really learn how to win at Facebook marketing, while everyone else is bitching and moaning and not posting. Algorithms are an intrinsic part of social media. They're always going to be here and they're always going to change. The people who acknowledge this and embrace the change are the ones who will win at social media marketing every time.

I put just about everything I create on Facebook – videos, blog posts, photos, one-line updates – because it allows me to *and* because so many people are on there. At the time of writing Facebook has over two billion monthly active users. Two billion! If it were a country it would be bigger than China. 1.5 billion people are active on Facebook every day. And five new profiles are being created *every second*. Them's a lot of eyeballs to get your content in front of. But before we look at how to do that, let's take a look at some of the so-called rules that have sprung up around Facebook and why I think you should break them.

THE FACEBOOK RULES ... AND WHY YOU SHOULD BREAK THEM

RULE #1: Facebook videos need to be short

There's an assumption that, when people are on Facebook, their attention span is only seconds long. What I would say to that is yes, attention span does tend to be shorter on Facebook, but if they like what they see, people are willing to stop and take a proper look. There's a myth that Facebook videos should be no more than one or two minutes long but if the quality of the content is good, people will watch for longer. It's all down to making a powerful first impression and capturing their attention but once you've done that, Facebook users will consume. Another thing to remember is that most people scroll through Facebook with the sound off. In comparison to YouTube, where 96% of people have the sound on, Digiday.com found that 85% of Facebook users had no volume on at all. So your first *visual* impression with a video is vital.

RULE #2: Facebook is an advertising platform

Nine out of ten of the band posts I see on Facebook are some kind of advertising. Even if people don't consciously think of Facebook as an advertising platform that's how they're using it. Of all the social media platforms, Facebook probably brings out the most selfish side of its users when it comes to marketing. There's a real 'me, me, me' culture; an assumption that if people follow or like your page they want to hear nothing but promotional posts from you. For me, social media is all about providing value and Facebook offers so many ways to do that, whether it be a 30 second silent video, a half-hour tutorial, a well-worded, thought-provoking status update, an informative image or a link to another useful website. Sometimes I think people are intimidated by all the options Facebook offers, so they just plump for one, like videos about themselves, and they limit the value they're offering. **Try seeing your followers as being part of a club**. I love using the word 'club' because it conjures up a warm, supportive and protective feeling and it makes you want to create content that will bring value to its members. If your Facebook followers feel taken care of they'll be way more likely to engage and share and attract others to your page.

TAKE CARE OF YOUR FACEBOOK CLUB AND THE REST WILL TAKE OF ITSELF

RULE #3: Video is the best form of engagement on Facebook

Video definitely isn't the be all and end all when it comes to Facebook and that's because of all the other possibilities Facebook offers. On Facebook we can use the written word and pictures too. Rather than blindly following the rule that video is the best form of engagement, **ask yourself:** *which is the best tool for the specific message I want to convey?* Would it be more powerful in a well-worded status update or a blog post? Would it be simpler to convey in a photo rather than a film? Experiment with different forms to see which gets the best engagement. Sometimes I've written a simple one line status like: *'If you could delete one entire decade of music, which would it be?'* This might at first seem like a bit of a meaningless update but it isn't at all. It captured my Facebook followers' imaginations and they had real fun engaging with the question and each other on the post. Today, I posted a similar question: *'If you could erase one band or act from history who would it be?'* Normally, I get a reach of between 1,500 and 3,000 thousand for my videos and between 500 – 1000 views. In the seven hours since I asked that question it's had a 15,000 reach and there have been 260 comments. That post has brought way more eyeballs to my page, which in turn kicks in the magic Facebook algorithm.

If you don't take advantage of all the things that are allowed on Facebook you're missing a massive trick. Keep your content fresh and keep experimenting. I'm not saying that video can't be effective but there's so much else you can be doing as well. And the real bonus of all this is, if you're terrible at video, you can capture your followers' imaginations with your written words instead. **Whatever your skill set, it will somehow fit into Facebook.**

RULE #4: Facebook is rubbish because of the algorithms

I know I addressed the subject of algorithms at the start of this chapter but it's such a big deal for people, I feel like we need to go into it some more. The fact is, **Facebook has one of the greatest algorithms that's ever been made** – that's why the platform is worth so much money. When Facebook first began and not as many people were on it, they would show you events on your news feed as and when they happened. But now it's been around for so long we all have much larger friend lists. The average Facebook user now has 338 friends. That's a lot of updates to cram into one feed. The people at Facebook realised that there had to be some kind of order of importance; that people would value certain posts over others – like their best friend's wedding over the fact that a casual acquaintance had chicken nuggets for lunch – so they created an algorithm to help prioritise things. This algorithm shows us the things they think we want to see. It uses binary numbers to build a picture of what and who we would prefer to see updates from. So, if you've liked someone's posts or visited their page a lot, it will make sure to prioritise that person in your feed. It's not Facebook dictating what we see, it's us, through our consumption habits, showing Facebook who we're interested in. If a post starts getting a load of likes instantly, such as a wedding photo, Facebook will class it as a life event and start showing it to more people. And if it continues to get more engagement, Facebook will continue to move it up the list and, instead of going to just 10% of that person's followers, it will end up going to all of them. That's why **the Facebook algorithm is a brilliant thing. It forces us to create really great content**. From a marketing point of view this is exactly what we need. If we choose to embrace the algorithm instead of resent it, it makes us do better.

RULE #5: Facebook advertising is crap

This is another so-called rule that I really hate! Facebook advertising isn't just good, it's the best form of advertising that has ever been designed. Ever. Can you tell I'm a fan? Let me tell you a story to demonstrate why I feel this way. When we started BIMM we had to advertise to musicians between the ages of 16 and 19. The most direct way of advertising back then was print advertising. And the best value for money were adverts in magazines that specialised in the musical fields we were after. So we placed adverts in magazines like *Guitarist, Guitar Techniques, Total Guitar, Rhythm, Bassist mag* and *The Stage*. Each advert cost £1,000. So we were spending £5,000 – £7000 per month. The age demographic of each magazine was 15–70. The demographic we were after (age 16-19) made up just 15% of the readership. So we were spending £1,000 to hit just 15% of the readers. 85% of people who would see our adverts would be the wrong people but that was still the most direct form of advertising we had back then. Fast forward to now, and Facebook advertising. You can't get any more direct. If I want to advertise to 16-year-old guitarists living in Manchester I can do exactly that. Facebook allows me to target an advert to a specific age and instrument and a five mile radius. And I often only have to pay as little as £20. The directness of Facebook advertising shits all over any type of advertising we've ever seen before. It's the most targeted advertising there's ever been – and yet people moan about it! If Facebook advertising isn't working for you it's not Facebook that's to blame, it's you. Imagine if someone drove a car for the very first time and they smashed into things because they didn't know what they were doing. What would you think if they got out of the car and said, 'This car is crap! It must be broken'? You'd think they were an idiot because it wasn't that the car was broken, it was that they didn't know how to drive it. **When it comes to Facebook advertising, don't blame the vehicle, learn how to drive it.**

Imagine if we could go back thirty years to before social media had been invented and asked people what they'd pay for a form of advertising that lets you get to exactly who you want to get to? I bet they'd be willing to pay huge amounts. But we get it for next to nothing and we're so ungrateful. We've become so used to having the internet we forget how amazing it is. I'm definitely guilty of this myself. Sometimes I'll be on a train and for a brief moment the internet reception drops out and I react like it's the end of the world. I completely forget that when I'm holding my phone, I'm holding a technological miracle.

RULE # 6: You should save your fun and unguarded updates for your personal page

This one really bugs me. Time and again I see business owner friends saving all of their best stuff for their personal Facebook pages. With their friends they're funny and unguarded and emotional and on their business pages they put on what I call their 'phone voice'. They're more guarded and formal, focusing solely on promoting themselves in a PR-conscious way. But nobody really wants to see that, or at least, not 100 percent of the time. They want the fun and exciting bits too. **When you have a separate business and personal page on Facebook you're in real danger of splitting your audience into two camps** – those you're prepared to let your guard down to and those you're way more cautious with. Then what tends to happen is that the people on your personal page engage far more because you're letting them in and your professional page becomes a tumbleweed zone of unliked statuses and zero comments. This often causes people to start sharing more of their business stuff on their personal page because they get more engagement there, but then you take away any incentive for your friends to like or engage with your professional page and you stop building the algorithm. Imagine if I said to you, 'If you ever need to contact me, here's my PA's number and here's my mobile number.' Chances are you'd never contact my PA, you'd phone me. Why go round the houses when you can go straight to the horse's mouth? People always prefer the most personal approach and this definitely applies to Facebook. I have a personal Facebook page but I only ever use it to keep in touch with what my friends are doing. I never post on there and if anyone ever sends a message to that page I always tell them to connect with me over on my professional page because that's where I spend the majority of my time. I try to treat my professional page as I would my personal, with a mixture of fun and personal and promotional posts.

If you'd like to get people to migrate from your personal Facebook account to your professional page try leaving your personal page dormant, with a note saying something like: 'It feels a little silly having two pages on here so I've decided to make my professional page my Facebook home. I'll be keeping promotional posts to a minimum and I'd really love it if you would connect with me over there, as that's where I'll be.' Do it a couple of times to remind people. And whatever you do, don't post anything fun or promotional on your personal page, as you'll negate what you've said and kick the algorithm in on the wrong page.

Facebook house rules

Whereas YouTube and the other social media platforms have certain house rules that you should obey if you want to succeed, the only house rule Facebook has is that there are no house rules. It really is the all you can eat buffet, where you can pile your plate high with whatever you like. No-one will tell you off for having Chinese food and curry on the same plate. And no-one will tell you off for eating with your fingers. In the world of Facebook, anything goes, which is what makes it so exciting. So let's dive in…

Greater understanding of your demographic

Facebook is the easiest of all the social media platforms to start building an audience on because you can start by inviting your friends from your personal Facebook page. And advertising boosts mean it's easier to grow your numbers than on any other platform. You also get engagement quickly on Facebook and because of that you can experiment with content and gain a greater understanding of your audience by seeing what works for them.

Facebook Page Insights is a brilliant way of breaking down the demographics of your audience. Don't forget, social media plays a key role in many different areas of business, not just marketing and the great insights into your audience that Facebook provides can help in all of them. You can find out what percentage of your audience are male and female. You can find out the different cities that your followers are from, and the age groups they fall into. From clicking the Insights button on my Facebook page I can see that 80% of my followers are men and 20% women. And 70% of my entire audience are male aged between 18 and 34. The Insights button also shows me that when it comes to engagement, 17% of the women engage and 83% of the guys. So when I advertise, I target guys aged 18 – 34. The geographical element of the Insights page also shows you where to target. Most of my 14,000 followers are in the UK, which shows me that people overseas aren't finding my page yet.

A great example of how Facebook has helped someone gain better understanding of their audience is a friend of mine who's a blues guitar player. He wanted to appeal to young women but when I took a look at his Facebook Page Insights it showed me that the majority of his audience were actually middle-aged women. This gave him a much clearer focus and he was able to create his content accordingly. Because I know that the majority of my audience are men aged 18 to 34 and mainly from the UK I know that I'm OK making references to *Star Wars* in my posts but there's very little point making references to the likes of Bing Crosby.

All of the things on the left hand side of the Page Insights are there for a reason. You can see the how many people viewed your page, how many likes you got, how many people unfollowed you, how many minutes of video were viewed. In the weekly overview it shows you the percentage increase and decrease in the engagement on your page. This is all information that can help hugely when it comes to understanding and satisfying your audience, but hardly anyone ever uses it!

Creating engagement

Facebook is excellent at building a community environment. It's also a great way of talking to your audience in real time – but this comes down to taking the opportunity to reply to comments when they happen. If someone engages with a post, try to keep the conversation going. Ask questions. It's a real opportunity to go out of your way to extend the conversation rather than stopping it in its tracks. When I engage with people on Facebook they engage back faster than anywhere else. I hate it when someone puts a video on Facebook and someone makes a comment like, 'this is amazing' and the person who posted the video just likes the comment without properly engaging. Imagine if this happened in a bar. Imagine if you went up to someone and told them you really liked their work and they just did a bloody thumbs up in your face and walked off! It's rude and disrespectful. Even just saying thank you if someone leaves a nice comment on one of your posts is better than a thumbs up.

Facebook Live is another fantastic way of connecting with your followers in real time.

What's good about it is that it feels more like an event than an advert. It also triggers people's inquisitive nature and makes them wonder things like: *Why is this live? What's happening? What's so important that you're broadcasting it in real time?* And, of course, *what could go wrong?* It's inherently more interesting. It's also very scary the first time you do it. When I did my first Facebook Live it reminded me of the first time I went live on the radio. There's no chance of a second take, so if you mess up there's nowhere to hide. Anything can happen and probably will. In the run-up to going live I was plagued by fears. I'd told everyone I was going live but what if no one showed up? What if someone trolled me in real time? What if I made a mistake? What if I wasn't able to answer their questions? These were all irrational thoughts because in reality, Facebook Live is just a conversation. If no-one shows up, have something pre-planned to talk about, have a title. And give it time. People probably will start showing up and when they do, acknowledge them and ask them questions to get the conversation going. Encourage people to comment. If the worst comes to the worst and no-one engages at all, the video will be there to be watched by your followers at a later time. By having a pre-planned topic you still will have given them value. If you get trolled you deal with it. If you get asked a question you're unable to answer there and then, tell the viewer you'll get back to them, either in the comments or a private message.

The first few seconds after I pressed the live button were terrifying but then people started popping up and I said I said hi to them and asked how they were doing and the conversation began. It was the most real, natural, fun and engaging experience I'd had on social media. I've done about fifteen now. The comedian Jason Manford does one almost every day. It's the best way of engaging with your audience.

THINK OF IT LIKE STARTING A CONVERSATION IN A BAR

I really can't stress the advantages of Facebook when it comes to engaging with your audience enough but so many people are getting it wrong. It can be really useful to use the bar analogy when it comes to great engagement. Before you post anything, imagine walking up to someone out of the blue in a bar and saying the thing that you're about to put on Facebook. What would their reaction be? If you just marched up and said, 'buy my album' or 'come to my gig in London this Saturday at 8pm', chances are they're not going to engage because you're not giving them the opportunity. It's like going up to a woman and saying 'my place'. You're not going to get lucky. You have to work harder. People are always asking me how to get more engagement on their Facebook page and I always recommend they put their potential posts through the bar test. If you were to say to someone in a bar, 'Do you go to many gigs in Brighton?' you've started a conversation. You can still sell your stuff, you just need to genuinely engage first by starting a conversation.

Excellent customer service

When it comes to customer service on Facebook it's all about value and how you're bringing it on multiple levels. Every time someone engages with one of my posts and I comment back, I bring value. Every time I message back I bring value. Every time I give them what they want based on their specific needs – which I've worked hard to identify – I'm bringing value.

Facebook gives us great scope to bring value. Don't be afraid to be creative when it comes to providing excellent customer service. One way in which I've done this is with competitions. Every week I run a competition using the hashtag #60minwin. Everyone who comments on one of my posts within an hour, using this hashtag, is entered into a draw for the chance to win a t-shirt, mug, Skype call or face-to-face meeting with me. I give away three half hour Skype calls and three half hour face-to-face meetings every week. From my point of view that's just three hours of my time but it provides great value.

I also invite musicians to send in their band merch to be featured on my weekly *Ask Damo Show*. Every week we have a featured band of the week. I can't over-state the amount of positivity this kind of thing generates on your Facebook page and amongst your followers.

Another way in which Facebook helps you achieve excellent customer service is through its Page Insights. It enables you to offer really tailored content designed to meet your customer's specific needs. It's also really easy for your followers to contact you via Facebook, either on your wall or via a private message. It provides great accessibility.

One thing that is definitely worth mentioning here and applies to other social media platforms too, is the importance of not getting disillusioned if you only have a small number of people following you. Sometimes people will say to me something like, 'I've only got one hundred followers on my Facebook page.' And I reply, 'No, you've got ONE HUNDRED FOLLOWERS ON YOUR FACEBOOK PAGE!' Even if you only have one follower to start off with, that's one person who is genuinely interested in you and your day. You have to treat them with care and respect. A small following is no excuse to shirk on your customer service. In fact, the opposite is true and it's actually a lot easier to provide excellent customer service when you have a smaller following. If you focus on really taking care of your one follower they're way more likely to recommend you and so your following will start to grow.

How you deal with Facebook reviews is vital to your customer service. I recently saw a company who didn't acknowledge any of their one star reviews. This creates a really bad impression to me. You're always going to get someone who won't be entirely happy with what you do. Your other followers will completely understand if you get the odd negative review, as long as you deal with them well. If you get a review saying you or your company is a pile of shit it gives you an opportunity – not to stick up for yourself – or pass the buck to another department. It's an opportunity to step up and take full responsibility for the problem. Personally acknowledge the review and offer some kind of solution in your comment. And make your apology genuine and heartfelt. This will make it very hard for the customer to stay angry. Equally, when someone goes out of their way to give you a five-star review, for God's sake acknowledge it, and not just with a like. Go to the effort of making a comment.

Branding through storytelling

The great thing about Facebook is that it allows you to tell all kinds of stories, whereas on other platforms such as YouTube you're limited to one. This is why I call Facebook 'the monster' when it comes to social media. You can do everything the other platforms specialise in and people will accept it. You can tell a ten second story like on Vine. You can create a Snapchat-style story. You can write a short status update like a tweet. You can share photos, Instagram-style and share videos just like on YouTube. All of the ways of telling stories on the other social media platforms can be done on Facebook.

Because it offers so much choice it helps to vary it up a bit. Facebook users don't want a one dimensional thing. YouTuber Casey Neistat is a great example of this. In my opinion he's one of the best storytellers of our generation but he doesn't fit into Facebook. His way of storytelling is very much suited to the YouTube way of doing things. He hasn't got the variety that works for Facebook. Therefore, at the time of writing, he has 862, 000 likes on Facebook, which undoubtedly sounds impressive at first, but when you compare it to the 7.5 million subscribers he has on YouTube it's considerably less. This isn't a failing on Neistat's part, it's just that he's not really interested in playing the Facebook game. YouTube is his platform of choice. On the other hand, Gary Vaynerchuck has 2.2 million Facebook followers and 850, 000 YouTube subscribers. His style of storytelling works very well for Facebook because he likes to vary it. He'll have a fifteen minute video of his day, an hour long keynote speech, a blog post, one line statuses and 30 second snippets. He's not alienating people by just doing one thing. The variety of his content is very clever.

Being seen as an authority

The different type of page you can have on Facebook, for example a business page, author page, public figure page or musician page, immediately gives you an air of authority. But this is only a starting point. On Facebook you have to be able to prove your expertise over and over again. Because we're living in an age of constant social media consumption what you posted last week will be old news. **You have to prove your expertise multiple times a week** so your audience can see that you know what you're talking about. They need to see you talking *and* delivering. If I'd just posted five of my *Ask Damo Show* videos on Facebook and left it at that they'd soon fade from my followers' memories. But because I've been posting them every week for fourteen months I've built a momentum. I have to keep on posting though, to maintain that momentum. So don't get complacent. Having a professional page on Facebook is just the jumping off point. You have to prove your expertise through your content every single day.

Going viral

Obviously you don't get to choose what goes viral on Facebook but the good thing is you get to experiment and improve. If you do one particular style of video and only get eleven views and then do the exact same kind of video and get only get twelve, and then do another and only get ten, the chances are, that kind of video isn't going to go viral for you. There's nothing wrong with a slow burn but if you want to go viral you can't keep doing same thing if you're not seeing an improvement in results.

Start thinking about *how* things go viral. What kind of things do people like to share on Facebook? What do they want to see? What kind of things do you like to share there? Look at what goes viral and then try to apply that to your posts. Think of ten things you could experiment with. If you want a video to go viral you need to look at every detail – the environment, the tone, the message. You can't go viral by just talking into a camera unless what you have to say is in some way outrageous or attention-grabbing. You have to make your viewer say, *I've got to share this.'* That's hard to do. Think of the type of videos you see going viral on Facebook. Jonathan Pie and his spoof political videos are a great example of this. They're all over Facebook because they're clever and funny and sum up what we're all thinking. Comedy tends to go down really well on Facebook when it comes to sharing. Although there's no secret formula, if I had to sum it up, I'd say you have to do something out of the ordinary that will resonate with your followers' emotions. Be funny, moving, angry or sad. Pull on their heartstrings.

FACEBOOK RECAP

- Facebook is an unstoppable force because the possibilities it offers are endless.
- Try seeing your followers as being part of a club.
- Take care of your Facebook club and the rest will take care of itself.
- Ask yourself: *which is the best tool for the specific message I want to convey?*
- Whatever your skill set, it will somehow fit into Facebook.
- The Facebook algorithm is a brilliant thing. It forces us to create really great content.
- When it comes to Facebook advertising, don't blame the vehicle, learn how to drive it.
- When you have a separate business and personal page on Facebook you're in real danger of splitting your audience in two.
- In the world of Facebook, anything goes, which is what makes it so exciting.

- The Facebook Insights page is a brilliant way of breaking down the demographics of your audience.
- Think of your Facebook posts as starting a conversation in a bar.
- Be inventive and creative with the different ways of providing excellent customer service.
- On Facebook you have to prove your expertise multiple times a week.

CHAPTER SIX

INSTAGRAM

"The way people communicate is changing … we are using images to talk to each other, to communicate what we're doing, what we're thinking and to tell stories."
Kevin Systrom, Instagram co-founder

Let's take a minute and think about the avocado. There's evidence that the avocado was present in Peru 15,000 years ago. The 'ahuacatl', which is Aztec for testicle (because avos grow in pairs hanging from the tree), was just another non-event of a fruit, ranked beneath the humble honeydew melon, until those beardy hipsters with their man-buns decided to do a Simon Cowell on it and make it the most important accessory of the decade. Seriously, ten years ago how many avos had you put in your mouth? Next to none, I'm guessing. But now even some branches of McDonalds have avocado toast on their menu, while certain furniture stores can't sell an armchair unless it features our green testicular friend perched jauntily on a cushion! And how is this related to Instagram? Here's a stat for you … over 3 million pictures of avocados get uploaded to the 'gram every single day. That's over 2,000 avo pics per minute! The same goes for the ukulele and gin. Two items the world had thrown into the bin labelled *'Get Fucked'*, until Instagram shone its marketing light on them.

If Facebook is about friends and family (according to Mark Zuckerburg at least) then Instagram is about relevance. Instagram is the difference between a meeting in Starbucks and a meeting in an independent coffee shop. Who wants a selfie with a plain old Starbucks' mug when you can get your 'Triple Venti Soy No-Foam Latte' served in an old flower pot, while sat on a beanbag? Now that, my friends, is truly Instagram-worthy. Instagram is a trendsetter. It's where we learn what the celebs consume before it gets filtered down to us normal folk; a bit like the jump from the Paris catwalk to the high street store. If Miley Cyrus says that it's OK to bath in cow's urine on Instagram, get us to the farm with a bucket!

OK, so I might be being a bit flippant here but from a more serious, marketing point of view Instagram is all about building trust through social proofing (social proofing is a psychological phenomenon of social influence, where people assume the actions of others to reflect and represent the right behaviour or action). Instagram also provides a great opportunity to create a positive brand and image. When it comes to social media, people want to feel as close to you as they possibly can; they want to get an insight into the real you. Of all the platforms, Instagram feels the most personal – or at least it has the potential to be. Apart from vlogging, your Instagram page gives you the best opportunity to show people an insight into your life and get your followers to engage. This is because people use Instagram to report on their lives from their phone. It's a chance for people to see life through your eyes. It's like being in the room with you.

At the time of writing this book, Instagram is a power-house. While Facebook and YouTube are busy looking over their shoulder for the next political shit-storm to hit them, the 'gram has its headphones on and is humming away, oblivious. Instagram's power comes from our consumption habits and natural tendency to nosiness. We're addicted to pop culture and getting the inside scoop. For many people, seeing Kim Kardashian's new bum implants is way more important than whether Donald Trump is about to kill us all. What's amazing about Insta is we actually pay attention to the channels we follow. When a picture pops up on our feed we actually see it, and this is especially true of the Stories feature. So right now, it's the ultimate marketing machine. However, I don't think this golden era for Instagram will last. It's bound to change on the back of Facebook and YouTube cleaning up their act when it comes to advertising. I think the fall-out will mean more ads on Instagram, which may well be a huge turn-off for users eventually.

As with the other platforms, Instagram has its own set of so-called rules, which – you've guessed it – I think you should break. Here's what they are and why…

THE INSTAGRAM RULES … AND WHY YOU SHOULD BREAK THEM

RULE #1: Limit the number of people you follow

Back in the day (which was a Wednesday) Insta users were protective over their feed, limiting the number of people they followed. Now, however, many Insta users follow hundreds, if not thousands of feeds in order to stay on the app for hours at a time. Following this many people means there's a whole new feed every time you refresh, full of pretty! The algorithm has evolved and Insta helps you sculpt your viewing feed according to your consumption and mood.

RULE #2: You should PR your life in your Insta feed

Sometimes it seems as if everyone on Instagram is trying to be David Beckham, using filters and photo-shop to make themselves as fit and tanned and perfect as possible. I think this is so fucked up because it's like living in a fairytale. Your Insta feed doesn't need to PR your life, it needs to tell a story – about you or about a moment in time. Instagram has made every person a walking PR company but it doesn't need to be like this. There's nothing wrong with wanting to show off your best you but don't do it at the expense of authenticity. Don't forget that Instagram was designed as a photography app to help people capture moments. It wasn't meant to be a PR machine.

Rule #3: Insta Stories don't matter

Whereas the Instagram feed is seen as the place for perfection, the Stories feature is often seen as the place where your posts can be more raw and rough around the edges. This is great but a negative side effect is that people don't utilise the story feature to its full potential. Often, your stories get more reach than the posts in your feed because they appear more prominently at the top of the screen. Insta Stories are such an easy way of doing a daily vlog and reaching more people in a personal, powerful way. This, in turn, is a more effective way of doing a sneaky bit of marketing without pissing off your audience. And don't forget that the content can be recorded separately and uploaded at a later date.

Rule #4: If you post it they will come

There seems to be an unwritten rule that because Instagram is a photo-sharing app, there's no real need for words or community building and as sharing is difficult on Instagram, many users stick to posting pictures and letting the hashtag do the work. But a lot of people, myself included, like to read the story behind the picture, so you should make full use of the description. Maybe the picture you're sharing only tells part of the story. Use the description box to tell the rest. Something that frustrates me about a lot of business' Instagram pages is that they'll take a great picture of their product or service or working day but they won't bother telling us the backstory of that moment or what happened next. If you've grabbed someone's attention with an image, you need to finish the job and turn them into a fan. Just as with every other platform, you are posting content to get a reaction and to find a way to capitalise on that reaction. Instagram is just as social as it is media. Community is a huge part of the 'gram and an area that anyone can benefit from immediately. Try this simple exercise: go and find ten pics that you like in the Instagram search and start a conversation in the comments just to see what happens. If you take the time to engage with others for a few minutes I bet you'll have at least five new subscribers within an hour.

RULE #6: You should post as often as you like

I usually say there's no such thing as too much content, just shit content, but on Instagram this definitely isn't the case. Posting loads on Instagram and clogging up people's feeds can really piss them off. We've all been there, haven't we? You want to have a quick scroll through to see what's going on but you're unable to because someone you're following has gone on a meme bender – or has posted their entire holiday album. **Over-posting does not go down well on Instagram.** Use the slide show, album or Stories feature if you want to post a group of pictures, that's what they're there for. Otherwise, I would advise you post a maximum of three times per day … and spread them out.

RULE #7: Hashtags don't need much thought

I think a lot of people forget that Instagram is also a search engine and they either don't bother with hashtags or they make them way too general. Think about it. Millions of people will use a hashtag like #beach. If that's all you use in your picture of Brighton beach, your opportunity to stand out in that search is minimal. But if you made the hashtag more specific, like #BrightonBeach or #pebblebeach your picture is likely to be more prominent in a search for those things. Equally, you don't want to make your hashtags so specific that no-one would ever search for them. For example #atthebeachwithmyauntyethel probably isn't going to be searched for any time soon. It's also pointless doing silly hashtags now. People don't bother looking at them.

Hashtags are also a great way of connecting with communities on Instagram. Research the hashtags used by the kind of people you want to connect with and use them on your posts. One recent change Instagram have made is the ability to follow a hashtag. This has made hashtags more powerful than ever because they'll show up in feeds of people who don't follow you.

Now, let's look some more at how Instagram can work for you…

Greater understanding of your demographic

It's very easy to tap into something and start building an audience on Instagram. This is brilliant but a word of caution – it's also very easy to tap into something and build an audience in an area you're not really interested in. Instagram is less forgiving than Facebook. While you can experiment with the form ie; stories, pictures or videos, you do have to be careful with the theme of your posts. Once you start a theme that works people will buy into it and they won't want that to change. If they start following you for your business advice they probably won't appreciate it if you suddenly start talking about nothing but basketball.

As long as you bear this in mind there's no reason why you can't build a great audience on Instagram and, if you convert your Instagram to a business page, you'll have access to Page Insights very similar to that of Facebook's. Instagram Insights lets you see how your demographic breaks down in terms of age, sex and location. It also shows you which of your posts have been the most and least successful. Personal pages on Instagram don't offer this function, so you have to get clear on who your demographic are first and then go after them, experimenting with different pictures and memes and stories to find out what they like.

••••

Creating engagement

It's very easy for people to contact you on Instagram and a great way for you to communicate back. And *how you choose* **to communicate back is very important. Instagram gives you the opportunity to create a legacy**. Let me give you an example. One day, a teenage girl called Katie was scrolling through her Instagram feed when she read a meme from the singer in her favourite band. It was a quote from something he said at a gig that had helped get her through a really tough time when she was in hospital. So Katie posted a comment below the meme, thanking the singer for his words and telling him how it helped her get through her operation. The singer replied to her comment, which didn't just make Katie's day – it's something she'll remember for the rest of her life and now she'll always feel a personal connection with that band. It's created a legacy and yet, from the singer's point of view, it took so little time.

Just like I said before about Facebook, it really annoys me when people don't bother to reply to the comments they get on their Instagram posts. People put artists, entrpreneurs and creators on a pedestal but I think it should be the other way round. We should put our followers on a pedestal because we owe them so much. It's never been more important to build a fan-base and community. Even brand new businesses can build a legacy on a one-to-one basis. **On social media you can do something every single day that might stay with someone for the rest of their life** and Instagram is the perfect platform to achieve this because it's so emotions-based.

Another great advantage of Instagram is the proportion of your audience who get to see your content. It tends to be so much higher than on the other platforms. When I share a story on Instagram, about 50% of my followers will see it. This is massive compared to the 10 – 20 % of YouTube subscribers who watch my content daily. And on Facebook, the viewing figures can be as low as 5 – 10% if the algorithm doesn't kick in.

Excellent customer service

Instagram is not the go-to place for complaints. People tend to take to Twitter and Facebook to do that. **Because of this, Instagram provides a great opportunity to create a positive brand and image**. It's a chance to spread love rather than clean up mess and fire-fight the negative. This is definitely something to be embraced. And you can embrace it by focusing on providing great content. Instagram also helps you provide excellent customer service by being accessible and keeping in touch with people. As you know, I'm a great fan of Gary Vaynerchuk, but I'm not a fan of his Instagram page because it doesn't have that personal touch. Most of the posts feel like they're coming from somebody else, advertising Gary Vaynerchuk. There's no real insight into the behind the scenes moments of his day. It's funny because I'd accept that kind of content on any of the other platforms but with Instagram I have a different expectation.

After trying loads of different ways to create value on my Instagram page I've come to the conclusion that the Stories feature works best for me and I use it to tell the story of my day. When I put a story on Instagram it's like I'm there in the room with you, talking directly to you and sharing my experiences. It feels a lot more chilled and laid back than my earlier, motivational meme phase and way more personal than the time I only used my page to share bands' posts. I think the key to providing excellent customer service on Instagram is to stop trying too hard and forcing or over-filtering things. Let your posts be as personal and natural as possible.

Branding through storytelling

Traditionally, marketing on Instagram has been much more subtle than on Facebook. It's a great way of telling a story in an instant. It's so powerful and it doesn't need the crasser, Facebook-style marketing. Instagram provides the easiest way to tell a story. Creating videos for YouTube is time-consuming and hard and vlogging can feel intrusive. Facebook can be daunting because the options are limitless. With Instagram you have one job and one job only – to tell a story via pictures or 60 second videos. The actor Chris Pratt from *Guardians of the Galaxy* is great at doing this. He's up to interesting stuff every day and he captures the moment and tells the story very well. He's also very funny. **The thing to remember if you're going to use Instagram to document your life is to make your life interesting.**

Being seen as an authority

Instagram is a really good place to be seen as an authority. What you share doesn't need to be educational for you to be seen as an authority, you can achieve this through comedy, creativity and beauty too. When you showcase beautiful shots of your products on Instagram you're still showing yourself to be an expert because people value beautiful things and the emotions they inspire. You can also build your authority through the story behind your picture. For example, if you're a writer you could post a photo of your latest book, with the story of what inspired you to write it in the description. But always think before you post. Ask yourself what impression each picture will make upon your audience and check it corresponds with the impression you want to convey.

Going viral

Instagram is probably the least effective of all the social media platforms when it comes to going viral because it's so hard to share another person's content. If you want to regram other posts you have to download a separate app and it's a hassle. For this reason, I wouldn't worry too much about going viral on Instagram, I'd focus all of your attention on creating high quality content aimed at your target audience and bringing them value. And don't forget to use searchable hashtags so people can find and engage with you.

Let's talk stats…

Instagram currently has 800 million daily users and Mark Zuckerberg is adamant that he won't stop until it hits the cool billion mark. Every day 100 million pics are shared and 300 million people add to their stories, which is almost double the entirety of its competitor Snapchat. So Instagram can be a marketer's dream. Instagram also has the highest interaction rate of any social media, even dwarfing Facebook and showing that if you can build an audience they are very likely to watch, listen and engage. However, there is one stumbling block. How on earth do you break through the noise? Here are a few tips…

Number One: Relevancy

While you can break the rules on Instagram, don't forget that the key word is relevancy. So, while you might not be a bearded guy riding a unicycle playing a ukulele and munching on an avocado, and like me, you might want to stick a fork in your eye every time you see an inspirational quote along the lines of; *'You can't get to where you are going unless you start with where you are…'* you have to remember people's consumption habits and on Instagram they like pretty.

Number Two: Unique

The pictures that usually get the most amount of engagement on Instagram are pictures that are in some way unique. From bizarre to outstanding, incredible to remarkable, or simply different. If you put nine shots in front of someone and ask them which one they noticed first chances are they will point to the most unusual picture, even if it isn't of the highest quality. People's eyes are drawn to something unique.

Number Three: Subtlety

Instagram is a lot more subtle than Facebook and if you use clumsy, Facebook-style ads, at best they will be ignored and at worst you will be unfollowed. Remember to bring value and be subtle with your calls to action. Be smart with your marketing. Saying things like, *'Link in bio'* or *'Scroll up for more'* allows the user to feel more in control and not bombarded by sales pitches.

Number Four: Tagging

Tagging yourself into a city, brand, shop, or even tagging other people, helps tell your story. This is all about being a part of the greater Instagram eco-system. Join in and be friendly and spread the love ... then watch it come back to you.

Number Five: Selfies

Studies have shown that photos featuring a face tend to get more engagement so, like it or not, people want to see you. That's what they signed up for after all. OK, so they won't want to see the same selfie, day after day, but they want to be kept abreast of your story and that story features you.

Number Six: Stories

Instagram report that one in five organic stories result in a direct message. Therefore, five simple stories done well should result in someone reaching out to you. Obviously, my advice to you right now would be to pick up your phone and make a story about reading this book ... preferably with an avocado if you have one hanging about.

Insta Influencers

Let me finish this chapter with this; an 'Instagram influencer' is now a legitimate job title. It's something kids aspire to be and done right, it's actually a very important and relevant job. If you want to grow your business or brand there's no faster way than the social currency of being promoted by someone 'hot'. It gives you that relevancy and trust and can be done in five seconds. If you want to increase your followers, my number one piece of advice would be to start to leverage whatever you can to get airtime and attention on other people's Instagram posts. Don't worry about trying to get in front of Selina Gomez's audience of 133 million, just focus on someone with a few hundred and don't forget that right now, everyone is an influencer to some extent. It's in with the micro influencer and forget about the macro.

INSTAGRAM RECAP

- Not using the description is such a waste of free space – grab the opportunity.
- Don't forget that Instagram is a search engine – use your hashtags wisely.
- Mix up your content, don't make it all about you, think about your followers and what they'd like to see.
- Over-posting does not go down well on Instagram.
- Don't take away all life and authenticity from your images and selfies with filters.
- If you build the wrong audience to sell your product to you don't have an audience.
- How you choose to communicate back is very important – Instagram gives you the chance to create a legacy.
- Instagram provides a great opportunity to create a positive brand and image.
- With Instagram you have one job and one job only – to tell a story via pictures or 60 second videos.
- Ask yourself what impression each picture will make upon your audience and check it corresponds with the impression you want to convey.

CHAPTER SEVEN

TWITTER

*'Timing, perseverance and ten years of trying will
eventually make you look like an overnight success.'*
Biz Stone, co-founder of Twitter

There's no doubt that in user terms, Twitter is still one of the social media giants but the key thing you need to consider when it comes to marketing, brand-building and customer service is consumption. These days, people tend to use Twitter for two reasons. Firstly, to get news – either local, national or global. Twitter is phenomenal when it comes to news. If there's a fire on your street you can go straight to Twitter for on the ground, up to the minute updates. Basically, if it's newsworthy someone will be tweeting about it and it's well worth bearing this in mind from a content provider point of view. If you make something newsworthy people will pay attention to it on Twitter.

The second reason people use Twitter is to complain. Twitter is the most used social media platform when it comes to customer service, surpassed only by email and phone. It's good to be aware of this fact in advance because then you can prepare yourself – more on this in a bit. Because of the customer service aspect, Twitter is also a great platform for listening, enabling you to find out what people are saying about you and your company with one simple search.

Smash and Grab

From a social media point of view, Twitter stands out from the rest because most people tend to consume it now in a 'smash and grab' way. They pop on, check the news story they're interested in or make the complaint, and go. Because of this there's far less chance that they'll see your posts and engage with them, so Twitter now feels very much like an echo chamber for marketers. The fact is, the original model for Twitter has evolved. It was supposed to be used as a way of connecting with other people and striking up conversations; an online office water-cooler if you like, but now there's way too much noise and too little engagement.

Twitter as email

Having said all of that, I definitely think there's a lot of value in Twitter, mainly because it's such a fantastic search engine. If I want to reach out to someone for business reasons Twitter is my first port of call. Like Instagram, it's another email-style social media platform but unlike Instagram, it feels more business-like because Twitter is less personal. It's a great way of finding people and sending them a message. It's a lot easier than finding their email address and it feels a lot less intrusive if you message someone via Twitter than say, their personal Facebook page. It's also completely acceptable to join in any conversation on Twitter. Can you imagine if you just wandered up to a stranger in the pub and joined in their chat, they'd think you were a loon. But Twitter feels like an informal networking event where everyone's free to join in, which of course, isn't always such a good thing!

Social proofing

Because of the search engine aspect, which turned it into a news and complaints forum, Twitter is also great for social-proofing. It's well worth keeping your page up to date and regularly posting for the benefit of the people who will look for you there. It can be a great way of proving your expertise and showcasing your work. It's funny because, even though all of my best content is on Youtube and Facebook, my Twitter page is where people will go if they want proof of my authority and they want to get in touch. This is probably because Twitter's able to provide this instantly. As long as you have a professional-looking, up to date page, with tweets displaying evidence of your work, it gives you an instant stamp of approval. You can tell someone's the real deal on Twitter within seconds. The way I tend to do this is through numbers. If someone has 20,000 followers but follows 27,000 it gives the impression that they've built this purely on a 'follow for a follow' basis. But if their number of followers is higher than the number of people they follow it implies that their content is of value and verifies their authority.

Follow for a follow

The whole *'follow for a follow'* thing drives me mad. This is where someone will follow your page, wait a couple of days, and if you haven't followed them back, unfollow you again. They're not interested in you for your content, they're only interested in increasing their numbers. If you do this, it means your feed is worthless. I once met someone who'd managed to get 150,000 followers using this approach. I think he expected me to be impressed. I wasn't. I just thought, *I don't believe anything you say because you're the kind of person who likes to cheat the system*. Following for a follow doesn't give you kudos. Ditto buying fake followers. People can easily see through this and you lose all credibility. Follow other people on Twitter wisely. I follow someone on Twitter because I value them, like the musicians I get to know through my meet-ups or people who have gone to the effort of engaging with me. Following someone can be a nice way of saying thank you. I want my connections on Twitter to be feel-good and genuine.

Building a following

The golden era of building a following on Twitter has passed, due to there being so many other social media options but it's definitely not impossible to build a following on Twitter. It does takes a lot of work though and consistency is vital. You need to post regularly to start getting any real traction. Think of it in terms of time invested. It might take you six hours to create a video for YouTube. Imagine the kind of traction you could get if you spent six hours on Twitter, building connections, having conversations and posting great content.

What you post

What you post is crucial. If it's nothing but self-promotional tweets it will be a massive turn-off for your followers. You definitely need to break the so-called rule that Twitter is a sales channel. If you're sharing something of value, such as the link to an educational video on Youtube, then it's fine to tweet a gentle reminder. But make sure you mix things up with plenty of sharing and conversational tweets too. As with the other platforms, focus on bringing value to your audience. If you do have something to sell I think it's far better to use an outside PR to do the promotion for you.

Be in the room

Because Twitter is an echo chamber you need to have searchable content and you need to be seen to be in the room. If you're seen chatting to people and retweeting and posting regularly about your day it shows that you are actually there. People will follow you if they think they're going to get you. Twitter is great for simple conversation because it doesn't revolve around pictures or videos. The potential for striking up conversations with people is amazing. Twitter is fantastic for the power of one but people don't take advantage of this and make the mistake of thinking that they have to market to all of their followers all of the time.

Another great thing about Twitter is the limited size of tweets. Even when the number of characters was raised from 140 to 280 in 2017 people seemed to stick to around 140. The shortness of tweets means you have to be concise and you need to bring your elevator pitch. It's also very time-effective – both in terms of composing and consuming.

Don't forget the hashtags

Hashtags can help people find you but because of the limited characters per tweet, you need to choose them wisely. Also, you don't want them to come across as salesy. Hashtags seem to be getting rarer on Twitter these days. It's very different to how it used to be. Using hashtags in order to be found seems to have shifted to Instagram. However, they can be great if you're trying to reach out to a community. Hashtags can also be great to hop on to when they're trending, especially if they're in some way related to your field. It's a great way of joining or inviting conversation.

Making connections

When it comes to connecting with others on Twitter **think of it as a telephone not a megaphone**, a two-way street. Don't stick your fingers in your ears and simply tweet about yourself. Look for ways to chat to other users and establish connections. It will take a lot of effort due to the changed consumption habits of

Twitter users but it's not impossible. In my experience, adding a picture or video to your tweet definitely improves engagement. As discussed previously, there are several ways you can find people, communities and conversations using the search engine and hashtags. You can take part in much bigger conversations if you're prepared to put the work in.

Turning the negative into a positive

People like using Twitter to complain because it's a public platform and they want to name and shame people into rectifying their problem. So, how you deal with any complaints you receive on Twitter is very important. I'm a firm believer in the fact that, when someone complains about you on Twitter, you can actually end up gaining brownie points rather than losing them – *if you deal with it in the right way*. If you take a complaint badly it tends to make things a million times worse.

The personal touch is great when it comes to complaint handling, such as tweeting back an apology and a commitment to fix things within a certain time frame. Showing *how* you're going to fix things also works really well. Sometimes people are afraid to apologise on Twitter because they don't want to admit liability, but that only makes them look heartless to everyone watching. 'Sorry' is a very powerful word and a great way to defuse issues. We all mess up sometimes and if you show that you're genuinely sorry and want to fix things, people can be very forgiving.

Dealing with insults

Of course, not all complaints are valid and some are downright insulting. A couple of Twitter users who deal with insults brilliantly are the singer James Blunt and the American burger chain, Wendys. They've turned insult-handling into a spectator sport because their responses are so funny. Here are a couple of examples from James Blunt...

Twitter user: *'@jamesblunt has an annoying face and a highly irritating voice'*
@jamesblunt: *'and no mortgage'*

Twitter user: *'I must be 1 of only 2 who genuinely likes every @jamesblunt song'*
@jamesblunt: *'nope, you're on your own'*

••••

Of course, using humour as a comeback can be a dangerous game. You have to be genuinely funny and self-deprecating, otherwise you'll seem rude. But handled well, receiving insults can earn you an army of new fans.

Pitfalls of Twitter

The searchable aspect of Twitter comes with some pitfalls too. What happens on Twitter stays on Twitter forever – it only takes someone to screenshot it. We're constantly seeing celebrities being caught out by tweets they made before they were famous. We're living in an ultra-transparent world now. I think this is a good thing because it means that companies can be held to account. But it also means that you have to be squeaky clean and very careful about what you put out there. Before tweeting, always ask yourself if it's something you'd want everyone to see. If you're trying to project the image of a blissed-out mindfulness coach do you really want people seeing your rants to Tesco about the price of their fruit and veg? If you want people to think of you as an authority on healthy living it's probably best that you don't tweet to your mate about the time you woke up in a gutter in Amsterdam after a weekend bender. Don't forget that people will be able to see all of your interactions – *from all time*. If you can't remember what you put on Twitter back when you were starting out it's probably well worth taking a trawl back and having a clean-up to avoid any embarrassment later.

TWITTER RECAP

- People use Twitter to find out news.
- People use Twitter for customer service and to complain.
- Twitter is a powerful search engine.
- Twitter is a great way of finding people and sending them a message.
- Twitter can be used find out what people are saying about you.
- People consume Twitter in a smash and grab way.
- Twitter is like an informal networking event where anyone is free to join in.
- Don't follow for a follow.
- Create content that's of value.
- Be seen to be 'in the room', making connections and having conversations.

- Use hashtags for conversations or to find communities, don't be salesy.
- Don't be afraid to say sorry if someone complains.
- Before you tweet ask if it's something you'd want everyone to see.

PART TWO

CONSUMPTION

CHAPTER EIGHT

CONSUMPTION IS KEY

'Think like a publisher, not a marketer.'
David Meerman Scott, marketing author and speaker

OK, now that we've looked at the technicalities of social media it's time to dig into what I believe is the heart of the issue: **social media is all about consumption and that consumption is constantly evolving**. This is a major reason why it's impossible to have rules when it comes to social media – our consumption of it is changing so fast rules can soon become redundant. But instead of resenting or fighting this fact, we need to embrace it. In this chapter, I'm going to show you how.

Technology is now evolving faster than the speed of light and we're evolving faster than ever as a species to keep up. We're also evolving as a society. We're more impatient and inquisitive than ever before, and our consumption of brands and content is changing rapidly too. The job of social media platforms is to keep up with our expectations and look after us as consumers. As marketers, we get angry when the likes of Facebook changes its algorithm or layout but millions of pounds of research will have been behind that change. It's all about improving the consumption experience. Google's number one job is to give us exactly what we want with one click. If we have to click on four or five links to get what we want then Google will feel that it's let us down. The same principle applies to Facebook. If we scroll through twenty posts and none of them are what we want to see then Facebook will feel that it's failed. Facebook is striving to give us perfection with every scroll, just as Google is with every search. In order to do that they have to evolve as fast as they can. The evolution of our consumption creates the evolution of technology to meet the demand.

Ultimately, it's in our interest that platforms make changes to improve the consumer experience because it helps keep our followers on there. Instead of resisting or resenting the changes, we need to find ways to complement them. When a social media platform makes an alteration try to understand why they've done it. Learn how it affects the end user and how it can improve their experience. For example, when Twitter increased the number of characters in a tweet from 140 to 280 your first response should have been, *how can this help me improve my followers' experience? How can longer tweets help me provide them with greater value?*

Social media platforms aren't for marketers, they're for consumers

This is such a key fact, I'll say it again. Social media platforms aren't for marketers, they're for consumers. So often we forget this and when we market to our followers, we don't treat them the way they want to be treated. Think about your own personal consumption of social media. How do you feel when your Facebook or Twitter feeds get clogged up with advertising? I'm pretty sure you don't like it. I know I don't. This is the great irony when it comes to most social media marketing. We moan about constant plugs and adverts when we're on the receiving end of them but happily inflict them on our own followers. Social media platforms build systems for the sole purpose of looking after their audience. To be a success on social media we need to take inspiration from that, not fight against it. Like the platforms themselves, we need to focus on how we can look after our consumer better.

Think from the end, not the beginning

To be able to look after our social media followers better we need to start by focusing on what *they* want rather than what we want. I do this with every business I set up. I identify the problem the business is there to help solve, then I work out how I can best solve it. Kind of like a Quentin Tarantino movie, I start with the end and work my way back to the beginning.

Whether you're a business owner, service provider or creative, you need to make looking after your followers your number one priority at all times. So many people get this wrong. They focus solely on plugging themselves or their product or service on social media, completely forgetting the fact that social media was not set up as a platform for advertising. When you work in harmony with the platforms and make it all about improving the consumer experience and keeping your audience happy, you really start to see positive results.

Move away from 'push media'

Most people are experts in social media from a consumer's point of view but this doesn't automatically make them experts from a marketing point of view. This is largely because social media marketing is so different from any other marketing we've had before and a lot of people are failing to realise this. When it comes to social media marketing, most people are posting adverts. I call this *push* media – constantly forcing things upon your followers. If you're doing this, you're only using a tiny fraction of the potential social media offers you.

The problem stems from trying to crowbar traditional advertising into a brand new platform. Think about the kind of advertising you see on television or in the press. All of these adverts push things in people's faces because they're a one-way medium. You can't have any kind of conversation or engagement with a newspaper ad. You can't share a television commercial with your friends. Before social media there had been no way for the consumer to talk back to the marketer. We're still advertising *at* people when we're now able to have a two-way communication. We need to radically rethink what I call push media and take full advantage of all the other possibilities social media offers us. If we don't it's a bit like watching the soap opera *EastEnders* religiously at 7.30 every night because that's the time it's always been on at, even though we now have the on-demand technology to watch it whenever we like.

It's all about engagement

A key strategy in social media marketing is engagement. If you can get people to like and share and comment on your posts it helps to spread your content. People can be really negative about their numbers when it comes to social media. I was at an event recently and during the Q & A a musician asked the following question: 'I've only got 500 followers on Facebook. How will I get on the radio with such a low following?' In saying this he's devaluing his following instead of recognising his hard work and the achievement of building five hundred people who are into his band. That's a lot of people. Imagine if they all came together physically. That's something to feel really chuffed about. But even if you had five followers on Facebook, I'd say the same thing. It isn't the number of followers that you should be focused on, *it's the level of engagement that you get from them.* And the level of engagement you get comes down to how you take care of them. If you look after your social media followers like they've never been looked after before your numbers should take care of themselves.

The people who engage with me most on my social media are predominantly British. I do have an audience in America but they don't engage nearly as much. The reason for this is probably that British people can relate to my accent, analogies and humour. Because I want to take care of the people who engage with me I regularly use British references in my content. I once made a video at Beaconsfield service station (which is like a mini village on the motorway). Any touring musician in the UK will have taken part in the long running debate over which is the best service station. A lot of people think it's Cobham but I'm firmly in the Beaconsfield camp and I made a point of saying so in my video. This got loads of engagement from my followers and led to a really fun debate in the comments. I deliberately wanted to connect with the British musicians who are engaging with me to give them a more fun and relevant experience. Yes, any Americans followers might have felt a bit alienated, but I made sure I addressed them in later posts.

You need to think of social media in terms of *the number of people who can make a difference.* That's the number you should be focusing on. Your followers don't have to be super fans they just have to engage with your content by liking and sharing and telling a friend. It's your job to make them want to do that. And you do that by creating content that will entertain, help or inspire.

How to help

When it comes to my own social media I see my job as helping people through my experience in building multi-million pound businesses, whether it's helping a bass player in a band or an international business looking to create awareness and target the right demographic to sell to. I'm constantly making content to try and fulfil that aim. I always try to bring value but every so often I hit upon something that really helps and creates peak engagement. Usually it's a message I've used before but wrapped up in a different way. I recently made a video titled

5 Reasons Why Your Band is Shit. The advice I gave in the video is advice I've given before but the title tapped into a common fear among musicians, so the level of engagement I got was off the scale. We will look in more detail at how to do this in the chapter on storytelling.

I also run regular competitions but instead of being lazy with the prizes and just giving away merchandise I try and think of things that will really add value to my consumers and help musicians who are starting out. I've given away a guitar and studio time. One time we even gave away the opportunity to play at a festival, which got tons of engagement.

The audience you want, think you have and actually have

Any good book or course on business will stress the importance of getting clear on who your target audience or consumer is. But one thing I've learned when it comes to audience on social media is that it's very easy to get it wrong. I break this down into three categories: *there's the audience you want, the audience you think you have and the audience you actually have.* When I first set up my business social media accounts I knew that the bulk of my audience would be students or graduates of music due to my background teaching at BIMM and ACM. What I didn't realise was that my audience would be so heavily male, or that the key age range would be 19–32. I thought it would be 16–20. When it comes to social media it's so easy to make incorrect assumptions about your audience and that's why things like the Insights page on Facebook are so invaluable. Remember my blues guitarist friend who wanted an audience of younger women but it turned out that the bulk of his followers were older? Make sure you don't fall into the same trap. You'll only be able to bring real value to your audience if you know exactly who they are and what their specific needs are. As I've become more aware of the in-depth demographic of my followers I've adapted my content accordingly.

The benefits of getting specific

It's good to have a specific demographic because then you can make your content more focused and powerful. If you try to keep too many people happy you end up not really pleasing anyone at all because your content is watered down. Answer the questions below to help you get clearer on who your target audience are and exactly how you can help them…

••••

HOW CAN YOU HELP YOUR AUDIENCE?

Your audience
- What is their gender?
- What is the key age bracket?
- What is their social class?
- What is their level of education?
- What is their problem or issue?
- What do they need help with?

You
- If you were going to do a keynote speech what would it be on?
- In what ways can you educate, inspire or entertain?
- What is your elevator pitch, based on how you could bring value and help?

Elevator pitch examples
An elevator pitch is one line that sums up what it is that you do. It can be really useful to create one to help get you focused. Here are some examples to help you...

Matthew Hussey: *Helps women have happy relationships*
Nike: *Help aspiring athletes achieve their goals*
Ed Sheeran: *Helps people with first wedding dances*

Seriously, out of all the wedding gigs I've done with my band, songs by Ed Sheeran are requested way more than any others for first dances. The guy is a first dance machine!

CHAPTER NINE

SOCIAL CURRENCY

'Activate your fans, don't just collect them like baseball cards.'
Jay Baer, marketing consultant and entrepreneur

One of the most valuable things you can do as a social media marketer is to cash in on social currency. Social currency is a concept derived from the work of French philosopher Pierre Bourdieu. It refers to the resources gained from being part of social networks and communities, both on and offline. These resources include gaining information and knowledge, helping form your personal identity and increased social status and recognition. Let me give you an example of how this works to make it a little clearer. Imagine a guy called Jim who's really into comics. This passion of Jim's is a defining part of who he is. So when he shares a photo of the vintage Marvel comic he just bought on his Instagram feed he's letting the world know who he is and he's gaining social status within the comic-loving tribe. He's also providing something useful and interesting for people who share the same values as him. That's why it's called social currency because it's something you acquire, increase and trade.

When it comes to marketing, a consultancy company called Vivaldi Partners defined social currency as the extent to which people share a brand, or information about a brand, in their everyday lives. A typical day in my office starts with someone putting the kettle on, then everyone comes together in the kitchen area. The conversation that follows is all about social currency as we talk about what we did the night before. Someone might say, 'I went to the new steak restaurant in town.' Someone else might talk about a film or TV show they watched. We share these things not just as conversation starters but to show our personalities and interests. We share to connect by trading social currency. Very few people will want to create a negative impression of themselves in this situation. We do exactly the same thing on our social media – we share what we want people to see and think of us. With every post we make we're trying to build our social currency with other people.

A good marketer will tap into this human need to trade in social currency by creating content that people will want to talk about and share. This is all about creating a strong brand identity rather than simply trying to sell a product. Nike doesn't just sell shoes. Their *JUST DO IT* brand has created a loyal army of people who want to be a part of that ethos. And more importantly, *want to be seen* to be part of that ethos. Their Air Jordan shoes are a great example of how they've done this. Getting Michael Jordan, the greatest basketball player of all time, to design and put his name to a range of their footwear brought a whole new generation to the Nike brand.

The Six Elements of Social Currency

Social currency can be broken down into six key elements, which make up a model known as the social currency wheel:

- Affiliation
- Conversation
- Utility
- Advocacy
- Information
- Identity

The goal of the social currency wheel is to explain how customers' social processes and behaviours drive each of the conversions to three different outcomes: consideration, purchase and loyalty. You can engage with customers during these social processes and behaviours and influence the outcomes.

••••

How to build the social currency of your brand

When we started BIMM a big part of our social currency was that we deliberately capped the number of students we would accept. Once we'd hit that number we said, 'sorry, no more' and we wouldn't budge. We didn't want to be known for being just another music college. We wanted to be known for our exclusivity. One day I auditioned a singer. She was fantastic but we'd hit the quota for our vocalists' course. I told her that we didn't have any more spaces but we'd put her on a waiting list in case anyone dropped out. Her dad was obviously a very successful person – I could tell by the way he illegally parked his Porsche right outside the door. He said to me, 'Surely you can squeeze her in'. The truth was, we could have. We had fifteen vocalists on the course and the room could hold twenty. But I said no because I knew that if we started bending things and letting more and more people in, we'd lose the social currency of exclusivity. Then he pulled out his cheque book. 'I can see this is a new business,' he said, 'and I know you're going to need money. Just tell me how much.' Clearly he was guy who wasn't used to getting no for an answer! At the time we hardly had a thing. My shoes were literally gaffer-taped together. It took everything I had to say no. As it happened, someone dropped out later and his daughter got on course anyway. But it felt great to see how badly he wanted her to come to BIMM. He obviously thought it was the place to be. We'd created the power of 'sold out'. We'd positioned ourselves as the best of the best. Everything was about the brand recognition and social currency. It's a bit like getting a first class degree from Oxford or Cambridge or MIT or Harvard. You're getting exactly the same as a first class degree from a university like Hull or Delaware but people will be more impressed because of the status these universities have acquired. That's a perfect example of social currency in action.

Capitalising on the social currency of tribe

When I started teaching at ACM we did part-time evening courses. There were a lot of 'weekend warriors' who came once a week for two hours. A large percentage of them were fifty-something-year-old men who were very successful in their (non-musical) careers. Often their guitars would be worth more than my car. Admittedly, my car was held together with blue-tac, but still. They thought a flashy new guitar would make them a better player but none of them were willing to put in even twenty minutes practise a week to get anything vaguely musical out of it. However, their money did help them with their social currency because when they bought the Eric Clapton limited edition signature Strat they were recognised as guitarists by friends who didn't play guitar. Even though they could barely play a note they still felt part of a tribe.

People want to be part of a tribe so, as a marketer, you need to use that to your advantage. You need to build a community that provides people with social status and connection. There's a lot of financial value to be had from making your social media followers feel like they're members of a club. When people feel like they belong to a club they tend to spend money in that club. The Canadian clothing company Lululemon have done brilliantly at this, cultivating an athletic wear range that is seen as the must-have brand when it comes to yoga. Because of this, if you turn up at a yoga class rocking a Lululemon top, it shows you're a serious member of the yoga tribe and pushes you up that particular social standing ladder – even if your downward dog pose looks more like a dead dodo. You're also highly likely to post photos of yourself in your Lululemon wear on social media, as another way of gaining that social currency.

Social media is the perfect place for people to identify as part of a tribe. Let me give you an example from my own life. I love the UFC (Ultimate Fighting Championship). When I was younger I got my black belt in judo and dreamed of competing in the Olympics. As a kid I'd wonder what would happen if fighters from different schools of fighting went up against each other, like a boxer going up against a ninja. The UFC answers that question. To me, it's the ultimate form of combat. The other day I saw a clip of ten top UFC knock-outs and I instantly wanted to share it because I thought it was cool. Although I wasn't consciously thinking so at the time, when I posted it on my wall I was also letting people know that I like this stuff; I'm part of this tribe.

Create a tribe people want to belong to

As marketers we need to tap into this need to be in a tribe *by creating a tribe people want to belong to and talk about*. Fundamentally, people are more likely to share something that makes them look good. So as marketers, we have to think about what that would be. **Our job is to make people look good.** Samsung are great at doing this. They have to be because they're constantly playing second fiddle to Apple. One example of Samsung smashing it out of the park was when they did a synch deal with the band Royal Blood just as they were breaking into the big time. Every time a Samsung ad came on in the cinema or online there was the band of the moment. This is the kind of content people want to be seen talking about. Samsung make content that their tribe will be desperate to share – especially if it gets one over on Apple. When it comes to social currency, Samsung are really on it.

Snarky Puppy are an unknown band to most people because they're very niche. They're musicians' musicians. They want to be the best of the best. Every time they perform their musicianship is ridiculous. A lot of it is technique for technique's sake but they do it in a very musical way, which is very difficult to do. If you post a status update saying you're at a Snarky Puppy's gig you're gaining the social currency of saying you're a musician's musician. When you see a Snarky Puppy video online you share it because you want to show that you recognise how talented they are – and this in turn makes you appear knowledgeable.

An example of a YouTuber with great social currency Peter McKinnon. He got one million subscribers in nine months because his film-making is off the scale. People want to share his videos because it makes them look knowledgeable about film-making by association.

The tribe I appeal to on my social media are musicians and the social currency I trade in is knowledge. When I make content the golden rule is that, as well as helping musicians, I want them to feel knowledgeable by sharing the content. I want them to go from taking in the knowledge I'm providing to teaching it to others. Even though they didn't make the content they're still helping and supporting other musicians by sharing it and this is how I want them to feel. I build my own social currency among this tribe by sharing posts about the bands I go to see. Everyone has a story of seeing a band before they were big. This is classic social currency. I saw Royal Blood with twenty other people in Brighton at the very beginning of their career. Now they play arenas all over the world. This makes me feel like I recognised talent early on and therefore I must be slightly cooler than everyone else. The truth is, I just happened to be in the right place at the right time. I regularly go and see local bands and that gives me currency with musicians because they see that I support the underdog.

Sharing another person's content still brings you currency

Sharing other people's content can also be a great – and free – way of building social currency. Some companies, like Lad Bible, only ever share other people's content. They've built a massive business without actually creating a thing. I often share interesting articles on marketing, branding, social media and music news on Twitter. Anything that I think will bring value to my followers. Even though I haven't created it, if I believe it will bring value by being informative, humorous or educational I will share it and in turn, help build my social currency among my followers.

You've got to make them want to share

As we've established, a big part of social currency is sharing – whether in person at the office water cooler or on social media. Therefore you have to make your content shareable. Avoid the boring middle ground that's been done a million times before. Stick to the outskirts. People will share things that they haven't seen before. No one will share the picture of your dinner from yesterday – unless you're a cannibal and the picture's of you tucking into a human brain. It's so important to think about this when creating content. You need to make something remarkable. This, to me, is the crux of social currency. You need to make people want to get involved with your business or brand. If they're not getting their social currency from you, they'll get it from somewhere else.

Personality types

Another way you can get people to share your content to increase their social currency is to tap into their specific personality. When it comes to social media and social currency it might not just be hobbies or interests that people want to show off, it could be their skillsets. If someone is known as the funny guy or the factual girl they'll be drawn to sharing content that reflects that personality trait. So make sure you mix up the style of your content to cater for different personality types to share. For example, a mix of funny images and top ten tips videos.

QUESTIONS ON SOCIAL CURRENCY

Answer the questions below to help you get focused on how you can capitalise on social currency in your social media marketing…

- **What tribes are you trying to appeal to?** The more you can narrow this down the better. *Lord of the Rings* is a broad tribe but if you follow

'Galadhrim of Lothlorien' on Facebook it shows you're a true fan and you'd gain real social currency amongst that tribe.

- **Is the piece of content you're about to share valuable to that tribe?**
- **How is it valuable?**
- **Is your content shareable?** Is it remarkable or has it been done a million times before? Can you make it more shareable by using creativity or humour?
- **Why would your followers want to share your content?**
- **How does it increase their social currency?**

CHAPTER TEN

SOCIAL MEDIA STORYTELLING

'Storytelling ... good storytelling ... is a vital component of a marketing campaign.'
Gary Halbert, author and marketing expert

Storytelling is a vital part of social media marketing and one of the best ways to build a tribe. There are three key reasons why storytelling is so effective when it comes to brand building:

- People remember a good story
- People will share a good story
- Stories provide connection in a way that old, in-your-face sales pitches can't

Think for a moment about the brands you find the most memorable. Chances are it's because there's a great story, or stories behind them and their products and/or services. In this chapter I'm going to take you through the five types of story you can use to build a social media following.

The brand backstory

There may be many different people or companies offering the same kind of product or service as you but none of them will have the same origin story. The backstory of your brand is what makes it unique. A great example of this is Richard Branson and the story of how he started his first business, a student magazine, at the age of sixteen from a public phone box. It's a great and memorable story and because of this people want to share it – like I've just done here!

When I was at a bloggers conference in Scotland recently I met a couple of guys who run a YouTube channel which is all about how to be happy by being healthy. When they started their channel they wore suits in their videos and were known as Robert and Steven. The problem was, they weren't standing out from the crowd of other health and fitness channels. Then one day, they made an important realisation – they weren't letting people see who they really were, they weren't making the most of their USP, the fact that they were Scottish. So they started calling each other by the names they used outside of their videos – Rab and Steve – they dressed in kilts and renamed their channel The Kilted Coaches. They injected the backstory of who they were into the heart of their brand and gained 50,000 subscribers in just over a year. This is the crux of storytelling and social media marketing – if you find an audience for your stories, monetising it will take care of itself because you will have built a loyal tribe who will want what you have to sell.

Ed Sheeran is someone else who has done a great job of sharing his backstory. We all know how hard he worked before he got a record deal; sleeping on people's sofas for two years and busking every day for months on end. Everyone loves a rags to riches tale like this. We want people to work for their success. We want to hear about the hard graft involved because it's inspiring. That's why a lot of people hate *X Factor* winners because they often go straight to stardom without having done the graft. People want to see the graft, they want to hear the story that proves you deserve success.

My own backstory has helped me a lot in my career, previously as a teacher, and now as a keynote speaker. The most valuable thing I brought to BIMM wasn't experience or business sense, it was the fact that I could personally relate to all of our students. I'd been in their place. I'd failed in my exams and band but had still been desperate to succeed. Most of the other people who worked at BIMM had achieved success in their music careers, some selling up to two or three million albums. They hadn't gone into teaching as a so-called failure. They didn't know what it was like to play working men's clubs two or three times a week and to play for next to no money. My backstory was very similar to that of our students. I knew what it was like to look around at my fellow students and wonder how the hell I was going to achieve success with all these other people fighting me for it. Yes, my fellow students had been my friends but ultimately we were in a fight. I knew the desperation and hunger and fear of things not working out. I knew what it was like to be prepared to work harder than I'd ever worked before but not being exactly sure what to do. My backstory gives me empathy with every music student I encounter, whether through teaching or giving talks in colleges. I know what it's like to drop out of mainstream education and commit to being a musician for the rest of your life. I know what a huge gamble this is. It's not like taking an accountancy course, where you pretty much have a guaranteed job at the end. A lot of people who've gone to music college feel as if they've failed their family by dropping out of mainstream education to do what is often perceived as 'farting around'. The fact is, you don't go into the music industry for money. You go into it for the love of music. That's why I was valuable to BIMM because, at twenty-three, I was so fresh from being a student myself and my backstory resonated with the students I taught.

Social media offers the perfect platforms for sharing your backstory. YouTube in particular is great for this, as are Facebook and Instagram. And keep your eyes peeled for trends that are perfect for sharing your backstory, such as YouTube's 'draw my life' trend.

The why story

People love to know and understand the reason behind something. They love the human story rather than the corporate speak because it creates connection and empathy. There's a why story behind every business but a lot of people don't bother sharing theirs. I think they're missing an important trick. The why story behind BIMM was that we'd identified a real need for a music college that looked after their students properly. ACM had gone from 40 to 750 students and we felt they weren't getting the attention they needed. There's a similar why story behind my new social media company, Black Rock Media. One thing I've learned over the past two years is that there are loads of people involved in social media who don't have a credible track record. The social media industry today reminds me of car mechanics twenty years ago. You'd take your car in to be looked at and they could tell you anything because they knew you didn't have the first clue. 'There are elves shitting in my filters and it's gonna cost me thousands to get rid of them? Oh, OK.' With Black Rock Media I want to put my money where my mouth is and show clients their return of investment rather than it all be pie in the sky. It's a results based industry and there aren't nearly enough people demonstrating proper results.

The behind the scenes story

By sharing the day to day stories behind your work on your social media channels you're building trust with your followers and helping them feel that they're part of your club. The bottom line is, people are nosy and inquisitive, they want to feel as close as possible to the people and brands they like. Imagine if you could have been a fly on the wall in Abbey Road studios in January 1969 when The Beatles recorded *Let it Be*. Back then that would have been impossible. But now everyone can take us behind the scenes, from bands to business owners to service providers and creatives. We all want to be a part of the 'I was there story', which is social currency to a tee. Provide your followers with these stories. Allow them to be with you, so that they can say, 'I was there'.

Hayley Williams from the band Paramore takes you behind the scenes on everything. It's like she's constantly thinking of ways to bring you into her world and I'm sure this is why she has two million Instagram followers. What I love about her Insta is that her shots are very real. It's not all, *'look, I'm on stage in front of thousands of people'* all the time. She lets people see her life through her eyes. She doesn't try too hard and she can be very creative and arty with her page. If I had to pick one word to sum up her Instagram it would be 'interesting'. The actors Chris Pratt and Will Smith are also great examples of behind the scenes storytellers. They regularly take their followers behind the scenes via their Instagram Stories in really fun and creative ways.

The products / service story

Sharing the stories behind each new product / service / creation you offer will help your followers to connect with them. They'll show the human side of your business. Even if your product isn't unique, the backstory and the why story will be. They make what you're doing memorable and shareable. This one is a real bug bear for me because so many musicians fail to do it and they're missing such a fantastic opportunity. Even if you're not a musician, you'll probably be able to relate to the following example when it comes to business endeavours and creations of your own…

The process of making a record is huge. You have to write the song, then arrange the instrumentation, then you have the pre-production process, where you go through everything with a fine tooth comb, from the tempo to which guitar you're going to use. Then you record it. Then you produce the artwork and finally, you put it out. But for some unknown reason to me, which could well be down to the old music industry rules, bands come on to social media and say '*Hey, guys our record is out!*' They thinks that this is where the journey begins. But what they've actually done is walk out on stage and say, '*And they all lived happily ever after, the end*'. They're only sharing the final part of the story. They've completely missed all of the build-up, excitement and anticipation. They've announced that the story of the song is finished without telling it from the beginning.

Part of the problem could be ego. It can be hard sharing the very beginning of a creation's journey. There's a tendency not to want people to see your work when it's rough at the edges and when you encounter obstacles. But it's precisely these parts of the story that build connection with your followers and make them feel invested in the finished product so, by the time it's ready to sell, they're desperate to buy it. People shouldn't be afraid of showing their imperfections. The reality is, if you were a fly on the wall during the recording of *Let it Be* back in 1969 you'd probably have seen that The Beatles made mistakes, argued and got frustrated. The days of so-called perfection have gone. And that's a good thing because letting people see your vulnerabilities helps them connect with you. The story starts with '*we're going to make something*' (whether that's a new business, product or service). If you start with that people will want to come with you on that journey – especially if you make it warts and all, every stop of the way. You have to understand where the story begins. You don't begin with the end.

Professional fighters are masters of this. Way before the fight happens they start telling us the story of how they're going to win. The story of mixed martial artist Conor McGregor fighting boxer Floyd Mayweather began a year before they set foot in the ring, when McGregor kept goading Mayweather with the story of how he was going to win. He did such a good job that many of us thought he might actually be in with a chance. Fighters create great '*Can they? Will they?*' stories. They bring in their backstories and make us feel emotionally invested. The actual fight is the conclusion of the story. If they didn't invest in all of the backstories the fight wouldn't mean nearly as much.

I shared the backstory of this book on social media for months before its publication. I made a YouTube video shortly after deciding to write it, where I shared the why story with my subscribers. Throughout the writing process I shared regular behind the scenes stories through vlogs and Instagram posts. Hopefully by the time it comes out, my followers will feel invested and engaged enough to want to buy a copy.

Your followers' stories

If you create content that taps into the stories of your followers and more specifically, the issues they face that you can help them with, you show that you understand them and build respect and trust. Casey Neistat's vlog about bike lanes in New York City was a great example of this. He tapped into an issue that many people could relate to and so the video went viral. You need to create stories that highlight your followers' problems or needs and how you can solve or meet them. This is a hugely powerful tool in marketing in general but lots of people don't do it, they just focus on the solution. What better way to connect with your followers than by creating a story that highlights their problem as well as showing how you can help fix it?

I did this when I formed my band The Indie Killers, although I didn't realise it at first. It was 2008 and the recession had hit. I'd been playing in wedding bands for ten years by this point and things had changed. People were skint and trying to put on events or weddings for less money than before. The tradition for these kind of bands had been female-fronted and large and playing mostly funk. It was a really dated model, which no-one had bothered to change. Then we came along with a three-piece, male-fronted band. *Sex on Fire* by Kings of Leon had just come out and it was the biggest song in the world. Most people who were getting married were in their twenties or thirties and the music they were listening to wasn't from the 1970s or 80s, it was guitar-based indie. They liked bands like the Stereophonics, Feeder and The Killers. We tapped into an issue – that people no longer wanted to dance to funk. They wanted to be transported back to their student days to escape the horrible recession. They wanted to relive their carefree days, having fun in the Student Union bar. The fact that we had less people in our band meant that we solved another problem – we charged less and therefore saved people money. As soon as we realised this we started highlighting the problems facing our potential customers in our marketing, in order to show how we could solve them. We asked people if they wanted a cheesy wedding band and when they said no, we offered them a solution. We showed them how we could save them money too and because we tapped into these issues, we started a movement and transformed the industry.

Someone who taps into the stories of his followers really well on social media is dating guru, Matthew Hussey. He constantly produces entertaining YouTube videos identifying the problems women face when it comes to relationships and how to solve them. He recognised a massive problem that had arisen in dating culture due to new technology. He tapped into a moment in time.

Grime artist Stormzy is another great example of someone who has tapped into the story of his followers. His work has a strong political message, highlighting the issues facing young people today. He's given his followers a voice through his work. He stood for something and channelled it into a solution and became a spokesperson for a generation.

Answer the following questions to get clearer on how you can use storytelling on social media to build your following…

- **What is your origin story?** What were the defining moments in your life that led to you creating your business / band / brand? How have you triumphed against the odds in the creation of it?
- **Why do you do what you do?** What is the driving force motivating you?
- **What behind the scenes stories could you share with your followers?** What interesting details could you let them in on?
- **What is the backstory of your latest offering?** How did it come to be?
- **What is the *why* story behind it?** Why did you create it?
- **What are your followers' stories?** What are the problems or needs that you or your products / services can help them with?

ADDITIONAL EXERCISE

There are a lot of great examples in this chapter. Go and research Matthew Hussey, Stormzy, Casey Neistat's Bike Lanes and The Kilted Coaches. Pay close attention to how they use storytelling to build their brand and social standing.

CHAPTER ELEVEN
TROUBLE-SHOOTING GUIDE

'If you're not pissing someone off on social media you're not using it aggressively enough.'
Guy Kawasaki, author and marketing specialist

I wanted to make sure that this chapter was as useful as possible so, before writing it, I put out an appeal on Facebook and YouTube, asking people to tell me the things they most needed help with when it comes to social media. Here are the most common issues that cropped up…

Consistency, consistency, consistency!
Oddsoul Sound

Consistency was by far the most common issue that came up and it can definitely be hard to maintain. First of all, set realistic targets that you'll be able to stick to over the long term. Start small and build from there. It's also really useful to have someone who will hold you accountable. Appoint someone as your social media manager. This isn't someone responsible for your social media, it's someone who will check that you're hitting your targets. Set yourself short-term, quick wins. Ask yourself what you can do to excite your audience this week. These will help add to the momentum. When you get positive feedback it inspires you to create more. Jot down lists of content ideas so you always have a bank to draw upon. Use the alarm on your phone to remind you when to post or create content.

Sometimes we need reminding to ensure that our content is ongoing. Stockpile footage so you can keep posting when you're not able to create. Don't take too long making things. Develop pillars for simple content that won't take over your life. Always read and reply to your comments. These can be a great source of ideas and inspiration. Scheduling posts is another great way of keeping the momentum going when you're busy or away. Remember that in order to make the end user's consumption the best it can be, the algorithm rewards engaged content. If you post at the wrong time for your UK audience because you're away in Australia the algorithm won't kick in. Scheduling your posts allows you to utilise the algorithm no matter what time zone you're in. Scheduling can have some drawbacks though, so I wouldn't advise you make it a routine thing. A funny post you scheduled a day in advance could suddenly seem insensitive or cruel if something happens to change things in between scheduling and posting. Your social media needs to be 'live' so you're there to handle things if need be. Finally, when it comes to consistency, don't make excuses. If you're serious about achieving success you need to make the time to post regularly on your social media.

> *Not wanting to release anything until it's perfect,*
> *which it never is.*
>
> **Dan Johnstone**

This is definitely one of the so-called rules that needs to be broken. It's so important to focus on the end user and their consumption. Content is consumed and spat out so quickly on social media that striving for perfection can be a dangerous game. It's the age old debate about quality vs quantity but for me, it isn't an either or thing. It's about producing quality content as much and as fast as you can. You need to find the tipping point between the best quality content you can make and the time-scales you set yourself. If your social media pillars are a weekly show, podcast, Facebook live or a monthly online gig then for consistency's sake, you have to hit these deadlines. **Consistency trumps perfection**. Anyway, who gets to decide what's perfect? It's so subjective. In the social media world, a ten second, badly shot i-phone video of someone's cat can get just as big a response as a multi-million pound advert for a blockbuster movie. The moral of the story is that it's all about the consumption of the end user and not your definition of perfection. Or at least it is if you're creating content for your audience. If you're doing it for you that's great, take all the time you need, but if it's for your audience you need to get on with it.

How do you start looking after your audience?
Alexis Ashton

Firstly, you create content that provides value for them. Remember that people are there to see you do the thing that you do. So, if you put out three pieces of content in a week, for example, an educational video, an advert and a new profile pic, then really you've only put out one piece of valuable content that week. Secondly, as simple as it sounds, you start looking after your audience by saying hello. Treat your relationship with your audience as you would any other relationship – spend as much time listening as you do talking, find out what you've got in common, give them your time and give them *you.*

I have a lot of followers but there's only a tiny percentage of interaction. I often feel like I'm shouting into the void.
Jay Stansfield

You summed up the answer to your question in your question – the reason you don't get much interaction is because you're 'shouting'. Imagine if you walked into a party and started yelling things at people. You'd soon get thrown out. But if you talked to people on an individual basis and started providing the room with value you'd soon be taken seriously. Remember to listen as well. Don't post a question and ignore the answers you're given. It's not just about you, it's about your followers too. Listen and interact rather than shout.

I'm nervous about Facebook or Twitter changing their algorithms and messing with something that works well for me.
Robin Nixon

I can guarantee that at some point this will happen. The platforms are entitled to change their rules and the only way we can deal with it is by altering our delivery to fit the changes. For example, when Facebook changed their algorithm to feature less marketing and more conversation from family and friends, the correct response would have been to post more valuable, engaging content and less promotional posts. The wrong thing to do in this scenario is to shout at Facebook and give up. NB: I cannot stress enough that social media platforms only make these kind of changes because they're trying to look after the consumer as best they can. If they don't, just like Myspace, they'll be gone. And if they're gone, so is your opportunity to use them as a marketing tool.

My issue is building an audience from scratch as we're starting a new project and feel like we're caught in a catch-22. No one is hearing about the project because they can't find it because the audience is small to start off with.

Kieran O'Brien

My answer to this one is two-fold. Firstly, you start off by inviting your friends and family. Even if that only adds up to ten people it's enough. If those ten people aren't sharing news about your project it's because you're not providing the value yet. You need to create shareable content and you also need to incentivise your small audience by looking after them like they've never been looked after before. If you make one person feel like the ultimate fan they will shout about your project from the rooftops. You just need one to get the ball rolling.

Secondly, you need to focus on distribution. If you want eyeballs seeing what you do then you need to go and find communities in the same field as you to start conversations with. That way you can begin sharing about your work but remember to make it conversational not promotional. Don't just start posting adverts in every forum you can find. Other great ways of boosting distribution are Facebook ads and influencer marketing – see the question below for more info.

How do I utilise the power of influencer marketing when I only have a small budget?

Tina McKenzie

••••

There's a belief that influencer marketing costs hundreds of thousands of pounds because these are the stories we hear on the news. But these kinds of figures only apply to the super-influencers. The fact is, everyone with a digital footprint is an influencer to some extent. Your job is to find someone in your core demographic who is a talker and leverage their influence. It doesn't even need to be for money. For example, if you're a spa owner and one of your core demographics are mums, you could reach out to a mum on Instagram with 200 followers because she'll definitely have influence with other mums. If you offer her a money-off voucher for your spa in exchange for an Instagram post you can bet she's going to shout about it. If you're a nutritionist offering an online course in healthy eating, find a respected figure in your field. Rather than looking for someone with a million followers, find someone who's looked up to on a more local level and message them and ask how much would it cost for them to do a shout out for your course. Even a nominal amount of money like £20 can go further than you think.

Talking on camera is my problem. How can I get over this anxiety?

Connor Wells

This one crops up a lot. Many people feel uncomfortable talking on camera and it's important to realise that there are plenty of other ways to communicate with your audience, such as the written word, audio and images. Imagine the photograph of a beautiful, hand-written note from you thanking your audience for always being there. It would be a powerful and personal communication that people would love. As long as you're bringing value it doesn't matter how you're bringing it. Choose the method that works best with your skillset. Some people are good on camera and some aren't and that's OK.

I'm not getting the reach I feel I deserve.

Steve Williams

I hear this one pretty much every single day and every day I do the same thing – I take an overview of the person's social media and discover that, without fail, the amount of content they're producing just isn't enough. If you're only producing three or four pieces of content per month you're just not looking after your audience properly. If you want them to look out for you you need to take care of them first. Reach comes from audiences wanting to share your content. So, unless you produce something ground-breaking and remarkable, you're reliant on the love of your audience. And how do you get your audience to love you? You post things that they'll enjoy and you engage with them. If you nurture the relationship they'll want to talk about you and share your content. Talking to someone three times per month is not nurturing the relationship. Love your audience and they'll love you back. Don't treat them as if they're in some kind of holding pen. If you are posting every single day and not getting any traction then you need to take a good, objective look at what you're posting and the overall appearance of your page. Is it conveying the right impression? And most importantly, are you bringing value? Experiment with different types of content until you find the sweet spot and begin getting traction.

How do I get my audience to do what I want, like buy my products?

Katie Bird

The most important thing to realise is you're not the emperor of your audience. You can't order them around as if they're your subjects. Your job is to build relationships so that when you do have something you'd like to promote they'll pay attention and get involved – should they want to. And they'll be way more inclined to get involved if you've built a good relationship with them. Building these sorts of relationships takes time. Patience is key but patience on its own is just waiting. You need to work like a mother-fucker, day in day out, and then patience will really start to pay off. Think of it from a consumer's point of view: how would you feel if someone who's paid very little interest in you ordered you to do something? Chances are you wouldn't be all that keen to respond. At the risk of sounding like a broken record, when you focus on building relationships and bringing value, the rest tends to take care of itself.

I just don't have enough time.

Matty Stern

••••

A lot of people get really daunted by how much time maintaining momentum on their social media channels will take. I really get this, it's something I struggle with too but I've discovered several key hacks that can really help.

Reposting

If I don't have time to make a new YouTube video I'll repost an old one on Twitter or Facebook. For those days when you just don't have time to create something new reposting is a quick and simple way of keeping the momentum going.

Scheduling time

I'm really disorganised when it comes to managing my time so about a year ago I decided to hand my time over to my PA, Katie. I knew that she would value it more than me. She wouldn't schedule a meeting for three hours if it only really needed to be one. She would make my appointments shorter to make the most of my time. Every week I tell her my priorities and targets and she schedules things accordingly. She also knows that I need a certain amount of time for concept and content creation. And each week we analyse whether we'll need more or less time on things. To give you an example of how my time is scheduled for social media, every day next month I'll have thirty to forty minutes booked in just for Instagram. I'll use this time to talk to people, like their pictures and post things. I'll also schedule time every day to respond to my Facebook messages.

I know that not everyone is lucky enough to have a PA to organise their time for them but you could try asking a friend or family member to manage just one day of your time to help see how it could be used more efficiently. Chances are, they will value it so much more than you. Today, Katie scheduled three half-hour skype calls for me back to back. At first I thought, *oh no, I'll have no time for over-running*. But actually it was really time-efficient because all three calls were over in ninety minutes. If I'd been left to my own devices I'd have given myself two and a half hours with space between for them to over-run. Another great thing you can do when it comes to time management is scheduling your day the night before. Work out your main priorities and list them in order, then add in how much time you're going to allocate to each.

Switch off notifications

For those times when you need to be in the zone and focused solely on your work, switch off your social media notifications so it doesn't feel relentless. This way you can get things done a lot quicker. But don't forget to switch them back on again afterwards!

I don't want to have to deal with haters.
Wimpy McGee*

Another thing that can affect your social media output is having to deal with haters. When you put your heart and soul into creating something and you receive negative feedback it can be really hard not to take it personally. Unless you're a psycho or a robot, people unfollowing or criticising or trolling you will hurt. Don't let it make you give up and try not to bite. Trolls want to get a rise out of you and they have nothing constructive to add. Like I said earlier in this book, whenever I get trolled I try and use it as an opportunity to PR myself and show the rest of my audience what kind of person I am. If I say something funny or considered in response to a nasty comment it shows I'm a decent person. Remember how James Blunt deals with online hate, using humour and intelligence to bat it off - and how well he comes across because of it. After all is said and done, you are going to encounter some kind of negativity on your social media at some stage and you're going to have to find a way of dealing with it. It helps to try and see the bigger picture. In the grand scheme of things, someone calling you a dickhead on YouTube really doesn't matter, even though it feels like it does at the time. Think about it this way, if you were driving and accidentally cut someone up and they called you a wanker it would all be over and done with and forgotten about in seconds. I know it feels more personal on social media, especially if someone is hating on something you've created, but you need to try and adopt the same nonchalant approach. You get used to the fact that someone at some stage is going to yell at you when you're driving but you don't stop driving because of it. Apply the same principle to your social media.

**As this is quite a sensitive issue and applies to almost all of us I may have invented the name for this one…*

••••

What if nobody cares?

Mark Hobson

For most people, achieving success on social media takes so much longer than they expect. It took the Kilted Coaches one year to reach 100 subscribers on YouTube but they kept at it and now they have 50,000. In the end, it's all relative. As long as you keep up the consistency and value you'll get there. And remember not to make numbers your target. When I look back on my life, I'm not going to feel proud because I've got a million YouTube subscribers. The thing that will make me proud is knowing that I helped people. If I were a recording artist it wouldn't be record sales I'd be most proud of, it would be what I'd actually created and how it had affected people. Focusing on doing the right thing according to your skills and experience and creating a body of work you're proud of is a far healthier, happier way to be. When you focus on doing what you love for all the right reasons it creates a great and infectious energy. When you're being authentic and putting out content purely for the love of it people will want to come on that journey.

Knowing when to quit

In conclusion, I think it's important to acknowledge that social media isn't for everyone. Although it offers many ways of creating content in different forms, if you don't feel drawn to taking photos or writing blog posts or recording videos or making podcasts then maybe you need to rethink promoting yourself or your brand online. You have to be realistic and know when to quit. The first time I had a session with my personal trainer at the gym he asked me what my goal was. I told him it was to look like Arnold Schwarzenegger – by tomorrow. I'd love to look like Arnie but I'm just not motivated enough to put in the work. Whenever my trainer tells me he's not going to be at the gym I cheer. I've accepted that body-building isn't for me – and that's OK.

CHAPTER TWELVE

THE JOURNEY TO SUCCESS

'We're living at a time when attention is the new currency. Those who insert themselves into as many channels as possible look set to capture the most value.'
Pete Cashmore, founder of Mashable

There's a model I use when I talk about a band or business' journey to success, which features three key points. The first is Point A, the starting point. The third and final point is Point B, which represents the end goal, the definition of success. What so many people don't realise is that there's a vital step in the middle of the journey. I call this Point A.5. Most people want to get from A to B with minimum effort but it doesn't work like that. **To achieve success you have to focus maximum effort on getting from A to A.5.** This is the stage where you grind out the work, day after day, for very little noticeable return. Posting regularly on your social media, building relationships, giving away content for free and doing deals and collaborations with others. If you don't put the work in here, the chances are you'll never make it to Point A.5, which is where you finally gain the momentum needed for success or, for fans of *Back to the Future*, you finally reach the magic eighty-eight miles per hour needed to power the time travel machine. Once you get to A.5 things finally speed up and opportunities come calling. In this chapter I'm going to share my tips and advice for both parts of the journey, so strap yourself in and get ready for the ride!

Grit and graft

To get from A to A.5 on your social media journey is a colossal task because you're committing to looking after people every single day. Most people only want to write the odd status but that's not enough. If you want to reach the momentum of A.5 you have to commit to being consistently creative and engaging with people, not ignoring them or simply giving the odd like or thumbs up. Being a success on social media is a relentless task. It lives and dies by what you've done that day. So even if you've killed it on YouTube one day, when you wake up the following morning you'll have to start all over again. It's never-ending. I did a video recently that I was really happy with but as soon as I woke up the following day I realised that I'd have to do another video just as good. When you create something fantastic you also create an expectation in your followers for more of the same. Think of your own expectations as a social media consumer. Personally, I love watching Casey Neistat's vlogs while I'm having my breakfast. If he hasn't uploaded something new I'll get in a bit of a strop and think something like, *Come on dude, get on the case, I need entertaining while I eat my poached eggs on toast!* Your consumer wants value and when you start giving it to them, they'll want more and more. So you need to be careful what you wish for, as it's a serious long term commitment. YouTuber GradeAUnderA is a great example of this. He rose to success with a video called 'Girly Drinks Versus Manly Drinks'. But then one day his videos stopped with no explanation. There was no precursor, no slowing down, he just stopped and all of his community, including me, became really concerned. Then finally, he posted a video explaining that he'd been suffering from depression and didn't want to make videos any more. The fact that so many people were so concerned about him shows how emotionally invested an audience can become once you invite them along on your journey. And they're not just invested in your product or content – they're invested in you. So be aware of the strength of commitment you might be creating.

Maintaining momentum

Social media marketing is like tensing a muscle. Anyone can smash it at first but it's very hard to keep up the momentum in the long-term. Pretty much everyone will feel the need to let it slip after a while. When it comes to creating content on a regular basis I liken it to being a professional songwriter. Professional songwriters can't afford to sit around waiting to be inspired, they need to pay the bills, they need to create on demand. To prepare for this they will have noted down ideas for lyrics and titles and tempo whenever they strike. Then, when it comes to creating a new song, they'll sit down and look through their list of ideas and use one as a spark. That's how I avoid getting blocked creatively – I'm noting down ideas all the time. Today I've written five new ideas in my phone. And in order not to run out of ideas I make sure that every week I'm engaging on social media. If I'm talking to my audience regularly they'll provide me with new ideas by letting me know what they need. It doesn't matter if you're a business owner, an artist, or creating a brand, the same principle applies. If you engage with your audience you'll create a cycle of you giving to your audience and them giving to you so that you can give back to them, and so on.

To create this cycle you need to make sure your audience are engaging with you and you do this by building relationships. If you talk to people they will talk back. When someone once said to Gary Vaynerchuk, 'It's amazing how much your audience love you,' he replied, 'I loved them first.' You have to put the love in first so that people will love you back and then it can go round and round in circles. **Don't think of your social media as another chore on your to do list, think of it in terms of relationship-building and providing value**. Don't sit around waiting to be inspired, maintain the momentum by taking action.

My social media business strategy

But exactly what kind of action should you take? When I set up my social media company I developed the following seven-step strategy to use with our clients. I also use it for my own companies' social media. This strategy can be used at any stage of the journey but it's particularly useful when you're starting out and trying to get from point A to A.5.

Step One: Research

The first thing I want to know is who we're making content for – what the audience's age, location, interests and secondary interests are, and what binds them together. I also get clear on what their stories are and more specifically, the stories we can help them with.

••••

Step Two: Strategy and Targets

As I mentioned before, Quentin Tarantino is famous for starting his films with the punchline then going back to the beginning, so you know what's going to happen right from the start. This is what I try and do with every business I set up. Before we plan a strategy we figure out what the big goal is, then we go back to the beginning and plan our route, reverse engineering the path to success. Next, I plan what kind of content we're going to create and where we're going to share it. Once again, I ask myself what we are trying to achieve. Are we trying to build an audience or sell something? How much time do we have? What kind of budget? How much content can we commit to putting out? It all needs to fit together. Then I create realistic targets according to the answers to these questions. When it comes to targets so many people focus on the wrong metrics, obsessing about numbers of followers or likes. Instead of making numbers your target **ask yourself how you are going to look after your followers every single day.** You don't need to be looking after your entire audience every time. You could do a one-on-one Skype session with someone or post an Insta quote or tweet thanking someone or follow someone back. Something as simple as that provides huge value. Simply clicking the like or follow button is a really powerful gesture and it only takes a second. I call this 'the power of one'. It can be so much more powerful to address one person specifically rather than a huge audience generally.

A big bugbear of mine is when people have a presence on a platform because they think they ought to but don't make any effort to provide value there. They'll say things like, 'I have a Twitter account just in case people look for me there'. But if they look for you and all they find is an empty shell it's not going to be all that impressive. If you're going to be on a platform find ways of creating value on it.

Step Three: Content Creation

I've said it before and I'll say it again, the first priority when it comes to content creation is to bring value to your audience. If you make this your focus it stops you creating content for yourself and it keeps your followers happy. You want to make the best content you can but you have to be realistic regarding your resources and time. How can you make the maximum content for the minimum effort? Create pillars of content that require minimum set up time. A good example of how I do this is with my weekly *Ask Damo Show*. I put a Facebook status up the night before, asking for questions, then ten minutes before we start filming the show, my assistant Melissa picks four questions we haven't had before and we're ready to roll. I can walk in from a meeting, sit down and start the show as soon as the mic's on. Melissa asks me a question and I answer off the cuff. Four questions in thirty minutes, job done. The show's very simple to edit and then we're able to break it into multiple pieces of content. This only works so well because answering questions under pressure is what I'm best at. If you asked me to write a blogpost in that time there's no way I'd be able to do it. So make sure you're creating content that plays to your strengths.

Also make sure that you're utilising all forms of content creation, including Facebook Live, Instagram Live and Insta Stories. Content creation is content creation, from spending twenty-four hours making a video to a ten second Insta story. It doesn't matter how long or short it is, it's all content. A simple tweet is content. It doesn't all have to be planned and prepared in advance.

Another important factor to bear in mind when planning your content creation is asking yourself if it's likely to get engagement. If not, add a call to action. Try putting something as simple as, 'Can I get an amen?' the next time you're making some kind of point with a post and see if you get more engagement.

Step Four: Architecture and Implementation

This is where we decide how we can break the content down, figure out where it's going to go and work on things like times, titles, descriptions, hashtags and meta tags. I can't stress enough how important it is to break your content down to maximise its potential. If I make a ten minute video for YouTube I'll also break it down and repackage it for other platforms. It's like I'm squeezing a lemon, trying to get as much as I can from every piece of content. I would never make a ten minute video and share it in the same form everywhere. But what I might do is share the full video on YouTube, take the sound off it to turn into a Spotify track, and use two or three soundbites from it for Twitter. I might give the video to a writer to transcribe into a blog post. I might take a still from the video to put on Instagram. I might use a sixty second snippet for an Instagram Story. This is another reason why you shouldn't be daunted by how much content you have to make. Often you can use one piece of content in many different ways.

When it comes to the timings of your posts don't be afraid to experiment. Remember what I said earlier about disregarding the industry standard? Everybody's audience is different. If you're selling to musicians you're going to miss the boat if you post at eight in the morning. But if you're selling to the mums of toddlers, eight in the morning could be the sweet spot. Find the best times for you and your style of content and your specific audience. Don't just follow everyone else. Another potential bonus of posting at quieter times is that it enables you to cut through the noise and get more engagement.

Another important factor when it comes to implementation are hashtags. They're an art form. The website Hashtagify.me can really help here. It tells you how popular a hashtag is and what works and what doesn't. It will also give you suggestions. Try searching hashtags on the different social media platforms to see which are the most popular in your field.

Step Five: Distribution

This step comes once we've posted the content on social media and it's all about getting more people to see it. This could mean promoting your content on forums, or copying and pasting it to send to someone, or boosting it on Facebook, or asking other people to share it. Effectively, distribution is all about getting more eyeballs on a piece of content.

Step Six: Engagement

This is where we look after the followers who engage with us by leaving comments or sharing our posts. It's all about building relationships and a sense of community. We reward anyone who engages by engaging back – and not just with a thumbs up. Remember, you're not there to thank someone for their comments, you're there to keep the conversation going. When someone comments on a post of yours think, *how can I keep this thread moving?* The algorithm will reward you for rewarding them. And your audience need to see that you reward engagement. Show the room that you're in it and let them know what they need to do.

Step Seven: Feedback

Finally, we do a review of the whole process. We look at what worked and what didn't and figure out ways to improve for next time. *Guitarist* magazine issue thirteen copies per year. Predominantly, the front cover will feature Eric Clapton, Jimi Hendrix, Stevie Ray Vaughn, a fender or a Gibson. The reason for this is that while there are hundreds of guitarists and makes and models of guitar out there, every time the magazine experiments and puts an up and coming guitarist on the cover they have a massive drop in sales. Even if they put Derek Trucks on the cover he won't sell magazines – despite being one of the most phenomenally talented guitarists on the planet. *Guitarist* have found their winning formula and they stick with it. You need to do the same. If something does well, do it again and rinse it till it doesn't work anymore. It's not about being varied, it's about achieving the reach and getting the job done.

Go through the strategy above and figure out which steps, if any, you are weak on. Usually people fall down on research because they make assumptions and end up marketing to the wrong people. Distribution can be another weak area because people think that once they've posted something on social media the moment has passed and they can never do it or talk about it again. Engagement can be another weak spot because people don't value it nearly as much as they should. Think about how warm you've felt when you've been acknowledged by someone you look up to on social media. It's a great feeling isn't it?

Preparing for success – the journey from A.5 to B

It's not in our DNA to properly prepare for success before we've achieved it. Hardly anybody dares to dream that. Which is ironic because people will gladly imagine what they'd do if they won the lottery. When it comes to aiming for social media success you need to be very careful what you wish for. Once you've become known for something it's hard to redefine things and reinvent yourself. I can't go from being music guy to rugby guy overnight. I've created an expectation that I'll update every day so I need to respect that. Ditto engaging with everybody. When your social media really starts working you will be in high demand. You'll also get hooked on the numbers and the need for you. So what will you do next? How will you evolve? It's a bit like the dreaded second album. You had your entire life to write the first one. But once you hit A.5 in the journey to success everything speeds up and increases. Expectations get bigger along with your popularity and you'll probably encounter more hate too. Then there's the fear of what will happen if it all comes crashing down. Basically, the second half of the journey brings a whole new set of worries.

When we started BIMM I had no money. As I said before, my shoes were gaffer-taped together. When I sold my share it made me a millionaire but I'd never been so scared of money, or rather, scared of losing it. When we started BIMM it felt like pushing a massive rock up hill, then it started to level out and then, as momentum really took off, it felt like the rock went speeding down hill and with us chasing after it yelling, 'Come back!' Basically, when you get to A.5 you need to strap in!

When you achieve success people will want a piece of you all the time and you won't be able to shut that off. You've put yourself out there, you've said, 'This is who I am and I want you to love me', but if it works it will come with certain constraints. The best piece of advice I could give you for this part of the journey is to stick with what you know. Don't let popularity tempt you into thinking you can be all things to all people. Don't let it go to your head. The fact is, when you achieve a certain level of success some people will put you on a pedestal and they might think you have the answer for everything. If someone comes to me with a question about music, social media or business I'll do everything I can to help but if someone comes to me with a question about relationships or mental health I'll steer clear because I'm not an expert in these things at all. The key is not getting too attached. In the same way that you should let go of any unhelpful negativity you receive online, let go of the positive feedback too. Use feedback as a guide, to help you see where you're going right or wrong but otherwise, detach. Just keep on doing what you love for the right reasons and the rest should take care of itself.

Right, now it's time to put everything you've read so far in this book into practise. It's time to burst out of your comfort zone and start heading for point A.5 on your journey. It's time for the 30 Day Challenge…

THE 30 DAY CHALLENGE

This section of the book is called the 30 Day Challenge for a reason – it will definitely challenge you to break out of your social media comfort zone! Before I created it I did a search online for other social media challenges and most of them were really lame, with exercises like: *'Take a picture of your work space and post it on Instagram'*. That's not a challenge, that's a basic instruction. If you want a thirty day introduction to social media you won't find it here. The next thirty days will be all about challenging yourself and different aspects of your personality and skillset. At BIMM we didn't just test students on their technical ability as musicians, we tested them on how they worked under pressure; we tested their creativity and their ability to think on their feet. I want to do something similar here. I want to help you identify your strengths when it comes to social media marketing so you know where to focus. It will take a bit of time and effort and some of the exercises may well feel uncomfortable, but if you rise to the challenge you'll find that these techniques will help you to build and look after your community very effectively. I'd love to hear how you're getting on while you're doing the challenge, so feel free to update me via my social media (you can find all of my social media info in the About the Author section at the end of this book).

DAY ONE: THE 'WHO ARE YOU?' CHALLENGE

There's a scene in the film *Jerry Maguire* where Maguire, a sports agent, decides to leave the cut-throat world of the huge, corporate agency he works for and set up a smaller, more authentic company. As he prepares to leave the office he declares his intention in front of all the other staff and asks who is with him. This scene sums up the starting point of social media for me – you need to use your platforms to stand up and declare what you're about and ask who's with you. So on Day One, I'm going to challenge you to get really clear on who you are and what you stand for. This is essential in order for you to achieve success. If you don't get crystal clear on what makes you unique you'll never stand out in a crowded market. Remember the Kilted Coaches from Chapter Ten? If you don't state what makes you different and show how you fit into the market place people won't be able to identify with you and say 'that's what I want'. The motivations behind your business or brand should shine through in every post. A strong message will attract a passionate following.

Today, take some time to answer the following three questions in detail:

- Where have you come from?
- Why are you doing this?
- Where are you going?

Once you're crystal clear on your answers to these questions you can apply them to everything you post on social media. These answers define you and will help attract the people who will want to go with you on your journey. Answer the following three questions to get even clearer. Don't cut corners in your answers, get specific. For example, don't just say you've been influenced by rock music, go into detail about the specific bands or artists who have shaped who you are today.

- What brought you to this point?
- What challenges have you overcome?
- What cultural influences define you?

Once you've answered all six questions in full go through your social media accounts and honestly evaluate whether you're showing who you are, where you've come from and where you're headed in your posts. What kind of first impression would someone get from your Facebook page or Instagram feed? Is it in keeping with your answers to these questions?

••••

DAY TWO: THE DEFINITION OF SUCCESS CHALLENGE

This may seem like stating the obvious but if you don't know exactly where you are going it can be a lot harder to get there. Getting clear on what success looks like to you is a vital first step on the path to social media success. So today, I want you to have a serious think about what it is you want to achieve with your social media. The most common social media goals are these:

- Social proofing
- Driving people to your website
- Selling something
- Building a brand or community
- Customer service

You can do all of these things with your social media but be aware that they all require different types of content, so to achieve success across the board will require a serious amount of work, resources and time. Where do your priorities lie? Are you motivated by money and numbers or are you more concerned with taking care of your audience and creating great products, services or art? There's no wrong or right answer, you just need to be clear. For today's challenge take some time to seriously think about and write down your answers to the following questions:

- What is your definition of success for your band, venture or business?
- What is your definition of social media success?
- How can you link the two?

By linking the two I mean, how can your social media success directly support the success of your business?

DAY THREE: THE RESOURCES AND GOALS CHALLENGE

This is an issue that comes up time and time again when I'm advising people on their social media. They want to achieve huge goals – higher numbers, bigger sales and a greater reach – and usually overnight. But social media doesn't work like that. Building momentum can be a slow burn and if you want to speed things up you'll need to invest time, man-power and money. Once you know what you want to achieve you have to be realistic about how you can achieve it. It's so important to set realistic goals and prioritise if need be. I can't stress this enough. You don't have to do everything, especially if doing everything means spreading yourself too thinly. Casey Neistat's main goal on YouTube is to create high quality films that tell a story. That's it. What is your main priority when it comes to your social media? And do you have the resources to achieve it? Let's get real today and think about logistics. Write down your answers to the following questions:

- How much time can you commit to your social media?
- How much budget can you put into it?
- Do you have the skill set required to achieve your goals?
- Do you have the necessary equipment?

If your answer is no to any of the above is there any way you can delegate or make changes to your lifestyle to turn that no into a yes? If the answer is still no you need to go back to Day Two's challenge and redefine what it is you're trying to achieve with your social media. If you'd initially said that you want to put out a vlog every day but now you realise you can't do that due to family or work commitments would a weekly vlog be more achievable? If you'd initially defined success as being prolific on all platforms but you now realise you'd be spreading yourself way too thin, pick one or two platforms to focus on.

Make sure you're not making excuses though. If you have a smart phone you have all the equipment you need to create quality pictures and footage. If you put down that you don't have enough time for social media marketing but regularly lose nights down the Netflix box-set rabbit hole then you need to re-prioritise. If you say you don't have enough money I'd urge you to really think seriously. This is your life and something you're so proud of you're talking about it on social media. Acknowledge that if you're serious about achieving success you've got to invest some money into it. And if that involves making sacrifices so be it. The fact that you bought this book is a good start. It shows that you're willing to invest in yourself and your success.

••••

DAY FOUR: THE PILLAR EVENTS CHALLENGE

As well as creating daily content I always advise clients of mine to design three or four events per year to build towards on their social media. I call these pillar events. A pillar event could be an album or a product launch. It could be some kind of open day or workshop to help people get to know what you are about. It could be a PR event, like having a sleepover party in a bed shop. The point is to create events in your calendar that you can build towards and create a buzz around on your social media.

I'm currently helping with the social media for a new music college called Waterbear. One of their key aims is to look after musicians and really help them with their careers. So we've created a PR pillar event – the Waterbear Tour. Essentially this will involve the team from Waterbear travelling around the country hosting events where musicians can hear talks and get advice from industry experts. But instead running a series of dry conferences in hotels, we're running the whole thing like a band tour. The events will be held in music venues and we're travelling around the country in a proper tour bus. By wrapping it up in this way we're making it way more creative and exciting for social media. And the best thing about it is it's not costing us a thing. Because we've come up with such a fun idea sponsors have jumped on board – literally. They see it as a great opportunity to get their branding in the venues and on the side of the bus. Not to mention the coverage they'll get on our social media. And speaking of which, the tour will provide us with months' worth of content – from images and insights to onstage and behind the scenes footage. When it comes to creating pillar events for your social media calendar it really pays to think outside the box.

For today's challenge I'd like you to download a calendar app or if you're old school, invest in a year planner for your wall. Next, brainstorm three or four pillar events that you could work towards in the next year. Are there any key dates for you and / or your product? If you make greetings cards Valentine's Day could be an automatic choice. If you have a new product coming out that's a definite pillar. Once you've identified three or four, choose the one you're going to do first. Ideally, you will have a lead time of about three months. Start brainstorming ways in which you could build momentum for the event on your social media channels. And remember to think outside the box. The whole point is to capture attention, bring people together and generate a buzz.

When I was at BIMM we tried to break the world record for the most number of guitar pedals used to play a recognisable riff. We got loads of students and Ace from Skunk Anansie to come down to Brighton Pier and we started plugging the pedals into two big guitar amps and a generator. We chose the riff from *Smoke on the Water*. Every time we played it we plugged one more pedal in. When we got to ninety-eight it sounded like a fart in a jar. We didn't break the record in the end but it didn't matter because the students loved it and we got loads of coverage in the local press and online. We pulled everyone together and got loads of new followers, while involving our audience. What world record could you fail to break?!

DAY FIVE: THE RESEARCH, RESEARCH, RESEARCH CHALLENGE

Now that we've got clear on who you are, where you're going and how you can get there, it's time to get clear on who your demographic is. In the back end of every social media business page there's tons of info about your demographic and your site. Especially Facebook. They've done an incredible job of giving you all the information you could possibly want and more. They let you know who visits your page, what gender and age they are and where they're from. You underestimate the gift of the Facebook Page Insights at your peril! For the Waterbear tour we used the Facebook Page Insights to identify where our demographic was and planned the tour venues accordingly. Instead of booking venues where we thought we ought to go, we booked them where our audience actually were, or could get to easily.

Let's get down to business. If you don't have a Facebook business page, your challenge today is to set one up, using your answers from Day One to inspire your content. If you *do* have a Facebook business page it's time to delve into the insights about your demographic, so that you can create content that's tailor-made for them.

STEP ONE: Go to your Facebook Page Insights and press the PEOPLE button on the side of the screen. This will bring up all of the key data about the people who visit your page.

STEP TWO: On separate sheets of paper draw three stick figures, ranging in size. Label your largest stick figure *Demographic A* – this represents the largest demographic in your audience (for example, women, aged 35 – 50). Label your middle-sized stick figure *Demographic B*. This represents your second largest demographic. And label the smallest, *Demographic C*, which represents your third largest demographic.

STEP THREE: Create a description for each of your demographics as if you were creating an avatar. For example, if it turns out that your largest demographic are men in their twenties, you could create an avatar that reads something like this: *This is James, he lives in the UK, he's aged 24, works full time and plays in a band. He likes going to gigs and is a fan of Star Wars movies.* If your second largest demographic are American women in their thirties your avatar might read something like this: *This is Kathy. She's a 35 year-old stay at home mum from San Francisco with two kids.*

I did this exercise for my guitar school, DK Music Academy. Our main demographic are mums who book guitar lessons for their children. I've called this demographic 'Lucy' and she's in her mid-forties and has two teen kids. Demographic B is 'Jeff', a 50-something guitarist who plays at weekend. And our Demographic C is 'Todd', a guitarist aged 14. We have about 1,000 Lucys, 400 Jeffs and 100 Todds. When it comes to creating content for our page we need to make sure we're taking care of all of our key demographics. Of course it's impossible to keep everyone happy, but if you get clear on who your two or three main demographics are and create your content accordingly, you'll also be creating a much happier and more loyal following.

DAY SIX: THE CONTENT BREAKDOWN CHALLENGE

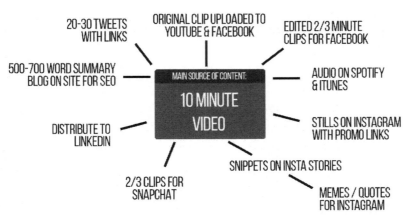

This diagram shows how much mileage you can get from just one piece of content. A ten minute video can easily give you one to two weeks' worth of content across a range of platforms, covering written, voice, pictures and video posts.

Once you've got your pillars I want you to create a strategy for breaking down your content and sharing it, depending on what platforms you use. What we're doing here is removing the need to make content for a specific platform. We're maximising content output and minimising time spent. Once you've got your strategy, set targets and start breaking down a piece of content you've made in the past.

DAY SEVEN: THE CREATE YOUR STORY CHALLENGE

Most of today's marketing and advertising revolves around storytelling. In particular, people are fascinated by stories that start with a dream, then detail the challenges that had to be overcome in order to achieve it. As I said earlier, I often use the story of how I overcame my failures at school and with my band and went on to found BIMM in my talks and marketing my different businesses. The best thing about your personal story is that it's unique. Most social media platforms have had trends that have tapped into this love of stories, for example, YouTube's *Draw My Life*, where YouTubers told their backstory by drawing pictures of their life. **Your challenge today is to find the best way to tell your story.** Whether written or in pictures or video form, I want you to document your story and attach it to your social media so people can see where you've come from and where you're going. This will emotionally tie your audience into your content.

DAY EIGHT: THE CREATE YOUR OWN HASHTAG CHALLENGE

Today, I'd like you to create a hashtag which is specific to you and can be used as a way of bringing your audience together. I have a couple of hashtags that have worked really well for me. The first is #60minwin. If my followers use this hashtag they're entered into a weekly draw to win a t-shirt, skype or face-to-face meeting with me. This works really well on Facebook for triggering the algorithm. The other hashtag I use a lot is #askdamo for my weekly Q&A show. This hashtag is used mostly on Twitter and allows people to ask me questions, or more importantly, it allows me to *find* their questions. Some days I get hundreds of engagements on Twitter. The hashtag enables me to quickly filter them for the questions.

Before you come up with any hashtags for you and your product, band or brand make sure they haven't been used before. If I'd used the more general and well-used hashtag #damo it would have been a lot harder for me to sift through all the tweets and work out which were for me. Once you've created your hashtag you need to find ways of promoting it. Tell people what it's for and what they get in return for using it ie; entry to a prize draw or the chance to have their question featured on your vlog. I did a talk at a social media conference in Boston recently and the organisers had set up a projector screen next to the stage showing a live Twitter feed. At the beginning of the conference the host told us that our hashtag for the day was #socialtools17 and our job was to get it trending, not just in Boston but in Massachusetts. They put the hashtag in the search engine and then every time someone used it in a tweet, we'd all see it appear on the screen. This in turn encouraged people to join in the conversation and by the end of the day the hashtag wasn't just trending in Boston, it was trending in the entire state. That hashtag created something awesome. It brought everyone in the room together and raised the profile of the conference state-wide. All from 100 people in a room.

Coming up with a great hashtag is a way of uniting your community. Create something that suits what you want to do. It could just be for a temporary thing, like the summit. It could be for a competition or an album title or a product launch. It could be a call to action like #freenelsonmandela ... or #freethenipple. As long as you make it clear what the hashtag's for and how and why people should use it, you'll be on to a winner.

DAY NINE: THE YOUTUBE CHALLENGE

YouTube is such an amazing platform and facility but it's so under-utilised by businesses and brands. Facebook, Instagram and Snapchat change regularly but YouTube rarely does and because of this it's a much safer platform. **So your challenge today is to organise your channel and start taking it seriously.** Arrange your content into playlists with banners and create a professional 'About' section. Make sure you're maximising SEO and pointing everyone towards your channel. If you're a specialist cake-maker from Philadelphia, making videos sharing baking tips, this needs to be in your About section so that its searchable. Then look back through your videos and change their titles to make them more eye-catching. Write thoughtful descriptions for each video, which include searchable key phrases ie; *'cake-maker from Philadelphia'* or *'how to ice your cake'*, and researched metatags (a metatag is a hashtag for YouTube).

There are websites that can help you research hashtags and metatags, such as tubebuddy.com but I would advise doing searches manually too to see what comes up. For each video you upload to YouTube you need your title, the first two to three lines of your description and the metatag to all feature the thing you want to be searchable, ie; *cake-maker from Philadelphia.*

DAY TEN: THE COLLAB CHALLENGE

I regularly spend time figuring out who I could do deals with, asking myself how I could use my skill, leverage and numbers to get something in return, like sponsorship or a collaboration. Collaborations are one the fastest ways to get your name out there because you're attaching your product or service to some-one else's influence and vice versa. You don't have to collaborate with someone in exactly the same field, you just have to share the same demographic. If you're a personal fitness trainer you could approach a local health café and ask if you could take a class there. Then you could film the class and get it online. If you own an energy drinks company you could team up with a haulage firm, with a view to keeping their drivers alert and safe on the road. If you're in a band you could approach YouTubers, asking if you could make music for their vlogs. **For today's challenge, I'd like you to come up with a list of people you could potentially collaborate with**. Be creative and think outside of your own field. When two completely separate industries collaborate it's a pure win win. Brainstorm your answers to these questions to come up with ideas for potential collaborations…

- Who shares the same demographic as you?
- What kind of social media reach do they have?
- How could a collaboration with them benefit you?
- How could it benefit them?
- What do you have to offer them?

It's worth noting here that when it comes to collabs it's a real numbers game. You need to approach a lot of people to get one in the bag. It's hard work and you have to be prepared to hear a lot of 'no's. But it will all be worth it for that one important 'yes'.

DAY ELEVEN: THE TEN TITLES CHALLENGE

The reason for this challenge is to get you to play the SEO game. A common mistake people make on social media is creating the content then trying to crowbar the title and SEO into it. You will get so much more traction if you reverse this process and think about the title *before* the content. For example, for the first six months I was making content every single day, I'd make a video on my bugbear of the day – the things that musicians did that annoyed me. And every day I'd think up the title after the content and usually it would be something like: *Stop Making EPs*. If I'd focused on the title first I'd probably have come up with something like, *5 Reasons Why the EP is Dead*. This is much better clickbait and much more searchable. People look for lists. They also respond more to strong opinions. They'll either agree or disagree but they'll want to watch it. **The challenge today is to come up with ten titles for content that you want to produce.** It doesn't matter if you're making performance videos or reaction or advice videos, the title is still the most important part of it. It's all about packaging your content in the most powerful way possible.

DAY TWELVE: THE 150 TWEET CHALLENGE

This challenge is probably going to have you scratching your head but please bear with me. **Today, I would like you to write 150 tweets.** I don't mean *publish* 150 tweets, but I want you to create a bank of tweets to draw upon that your audience will value. The reason for this exercise is to get you to think outside of the box and be creative. You can't just write 150 tweets saying 'buy my book / record / product'. The act of writing so many in one go will force you to be more varied and bring more value. Here are some suggestions for categories to help you:

Create different tweets for your different demographics

Using the challenge from Day 5, when you identified your key demographics, compose a series of tweets aimed specifically at each group, remembering to ask yourself, *what would bring them value?*

••••

Share old content

A lot of people will create a really great blog or vlog and only ever tweet about it once. This is such a waste of hard work. Chances are, the majority of your followers didn't see it first time round, so don't be afraid of sharing something more than once. But if you do repost something, share it in a way that's fresh and new and definitely don't apologise for sharing it again, especially if it's content that helps. Post it as if you're posting it for the very first time.

Conversation starters

Use some of your 150 tweets to ask people for their opinion or feedback on something. Try using the Twitter poll option to get them involved. Tweet directly to other people. Make Twitter a two-way thing by asking and answering questions. Who could you engage with on your Twitter feed? Who could you thank? Thanking a public figure could be a great way of engaging your followers if they like that person too. Conversational tweets make a refreshing change from the self-promotional.

Share someone else's content

Incorporate someone else's post into your own story. For example, share an article about someone who has really influenced you and talk about how they've influenced you in your tweet. Or share an amazing video and tell your followers what it is you love about it. Remember that sharing gives you social currency.

Promotional

The rule of thirds is a big thing on twitter. Everything you post should fall into three equal categories: *promotion*, *sharing* and *conversation*. This is a great guide to make sure your twitter stream stays in balance. It's absolutely fine for some of your 150 tweets to be promoting you and your work, just make sure it isn't more than a third.

DAY THIRTEEN: THE ASK CHALLENGE

I've got a nice easy one for you today. **I want you to talk to your audience and ask them what they most value about your socials.** Audience research is so valuable. Today we're going to stop preaching, marketing and selling and ask their advice. And I'm not talking about a status update or picture or video. I want you to do this one to one. I want you to message individual people who like your page and ask them for their help. People like to help so they should respond positively. Tell them that you want to provide them and the rest of your audience with as much value as you can and with that in mind, you'd love to know what content of yours they value the most and what they value the least. Also ask them what you could do on your socials to make their life just that little bit better. Pay close attention to the feedback you get and sculpt your social media accordingly.

DAY FOURTEEN: THE WRITTEN CHALLENGE

This is a test to see if your writing style excites your audience. Everyone has a different writing style. Because I'm nervous about writing I try and bring humour into it, so that if someone criticises my writing I can laugh it off and say I wasn't being serious. This tends to work for my audience. **Today, I want you to write something for your social media and see what kind of reaction and engagement you get.** If you normally put out pictures or videos how does the audience reaction differ? You don't have to write a full blog post. You could write a longer than usual Facebook post, or share a photo of something you've hand-written. People value text more than you might think because they see how much time and thought has gone into it. It's a bit like the difference between receiving a handwritten letter and a text message. Interestingly, I tend to get separate groups of people engaging with my written and video content. Mixing it up enables you to engage with the most amount of people.

DAY FIFTEEN: THE TIME-FRAME CHALLENGE

Taking a normal piece of content but adding a time limit radically changes what you're putting out and how it's consumed. For example, if you say you're going to document yourself writing a poem in five minutes, you've automatically made it more interesting and consumable. Or if you tell your followers you're going to do a Q&A for just two minutes, you've put a tiny spin on it which makes it all that more exciting. **Your challenge today is to make a piece of content and**

specifically add a time limit that's unrealistic. This should make it funny and interesting, not to mention creative!

DAY SIXTEEN: THE INSTA STORY HIGHLIGHT CHALLENGE

Instagram have a new feature where you can save stories as highlights. So if you've done something you're really proud of, you can save it as a highlight on your profile and it won't disappear after twenty-four hours like a normal Insta Story. You should definitely take advantage of this feature to help bring your Instagram profile to life. **Today's challenge is to plan an Insta Story that you can save as a highlight.** Make it something special that will add value and interest to your page.

DAY SEVENTEEN: THE GIVE AWAY SOMETHING OF MEANING CHALLENGE

Everyone knows that offers and competitions work really well on social media but most people try and give away the least amount possible. Or if they do give away something really good, they stretch the competition over such a long time period that the consumer loses interest. A good rule of thumb when it comes to social media giveaways is that the prize should match the action or effort required on the part of the consumer. For example, a band t-shirt worth £6 is a great giveaway for followers who comment and share your hashtag and help kick-start the Facebook algorithm. **But for today's challenge I want you to consider giving away something of meaning, something that really shows how much you value your audience.** If you're in a band, instead of giving away an album or t-shirt, why don't you give away one of your guitars? A prize like that instantly triggers emotion. I'm not expecting you to give away your treasured 1970s Strat; the prize you offer doesn't have to be expensive but it's got to have meaning. After I had a chat about this with musician Connor Wells he gave away one of his acoustic guitars. It was worth about £100 but so much more in terms of meaning. Not only did he get more engagement than ever before on his social media but I mention this story about twice a week – and now I'm talking about it in this book. I'm constantly spreading the word about Connor and his music because of what he did.

I ran a prize draw the first week after publishing this book. Everyone who bought the book and sent me a copy of their receipt got entered into a draw for the prize of three months of one-to-one consultations on their social media with me and my team. A prize worth £20,000. The reason I did that was to create excitement about the book in my audience and to do that I had to do something ridiculously big in comparison to what the audience were giving me.

What could you give away to show your audience how much you value them? If you're an artist, could you create a piece specifically for someone to win as a competition prize? If you provide some kind of service could you create a bespoke package as a prize? What better way to show your audience you appreciate them than by pouring time and effort into something for them? Once you've decided upon your prize make a video or write a post about it, so people can see exactly how much it means to you. Make sure that the call to action benefits you and them. For example, they get entered into a prize draw if they share one of your posts using the competition hashtag. Have a time limit of no longer than a week so people don't become bored or disengaged. It might also be worth boosting your competition post on Facebook – but only to your existing audience. You're rewarding their loyalty with this prize rather than trying to build a new audience.

DAY EIGHTEEN: THE FACEBOOK LIVE CHALLENGE

Most people I talk to haven't even tried Facebook Live because the thought is too terrifying. But what's terrifying to the user is exactly what makes it so exciting to the consumer. The fact that something can and possibly will go wrong is a key reason why people will tune in. But the huge benefit of Facebook Live is that it injects real-life excitement and risk into your social media. And it gives you the ability to think on your feet. If things do go hideously wrong you can delete it so it's not there forever, even if some people will have seen it. The trick is to not overthink your Facebook Live, planning it all out meticulously beforehand. Sometimes it's nice to just be there and allow people to talk to you as if you're having a Skype call. Another tip is to have something to talk about during the first twenty seconds or so, when you're waiting for people to join you. That way, when people watch the recording later, there will be content from the start, not you just staring into the camera. If you go on and nobody turns up, just leave and try again another time. It really doesn't matter. As soon as someone does turn up say hello to them and ask them a question. Right away you'll be in a conversation. I've never done a Facebook Live that's been silent. As soon as you start chatting to someone others will join in. It's brilliant for getting engagement and does wonders for your algorithm. Plus it leaves you with a video on your feed – a piece of content that you'd never be able to recreate due to the live element. So, today's challenge? You've guessed it – do a Facebook Live!

DAY NINETEEN: THE EMAIL NEWSLETTER CHALLENGE

Whilst a newsletter is not technically social media, your social media should be subtly pushing your audience into the places you want them to go, so you can give them more value. Social media can be a great way to build excitement about your newsletter, enabling you to bring your audience value via email. There are plenty of free newsletter distribution services like MailChimp. And don't worry about having to spend loads of time and money to make it look beautiful, the modern trend is to make your newsletter look way more like a simple email. You don't have to be heavy on content either. Just a couple of paragraphs will do. Newsletters should be more about bringing value than salesy and because of that you can create a really simple newsletter in less than an hour. Imagine getting a newsletter from your favourite YouTuber, sports star or entrepreneur that reads just like a personal email, telling you the story of their day. You're excited, you've got value, you're interested and you're warmed up. And it's so simple.

Your challenge today is to start an email newsletter. If you already have one I want you to think of what you could offer to get more people to sign up. I'm currently offering people the chance to take part in this 30 Day Challenge if they sign up for my newsletter. I've made videos for each of the days and once they've signed up they'll automatically get a video per day for the next thirty days. I'm also giving them three chapters of this book for free.

DAY TWENTY: THE AUDIO CHALLENGE

With the introduction of voice recognition, AI audio has become a key player in online marketing. If you think about it in terms of consumption, so much of the social media that you consume is visual. Tweets, blogs, videos, pictures, all require you to *view* the content, which means there are huge chunks of time when you aren't able consume these things. When you're at the gym, driving a car, doing tasks like washing up, all of these forms of social media are off-limits. But stick your earplugs in and you absolutely can listen to audio content. So, turning it back to a marketing point of view, it makes perfect sense to start creating content that people can listen to. Podcasting is a rapidly growing medium and there are several accessible platforms, such as Spotify, Google Play and SoundCloud, where you can make a start instantly. It can literally be as simple as pressing record on the voice recorder on your phone, talking into it and sending the recording straight to the platform. Bonus tip: If you upload audio to SoundCloud you're automatically given an RSS code, which is what you need to get your audio on i-tunes. You can also connect your SoundCloud account to i-tunes, so that it automatically uploads to both platforms.

Your challenge today is to create a piece of audio content and upload it to at least one audio platform and from there, share it to your other social media platforms, telling people you now have a podcast / audio-based platform available. Take note of how your audience react, so you can decide whether or not to carry on.

DAY TWENTY-ONE: THE YOUTUBE COLLAB CHALLENGE

The reason I've created a separate collaboration challenge for YouTube is because the type of person you're going to partner up with here will probably need to be video-based. **Your challenge for today is to think about who you could collaborate with on YouTube and what kind of content you could put out.** Ask your audience for ideas. Then contact the person and try to set up a collab for as soon as possible. Remember that this isn't about gaining numbers, it's about doing something interesting for your audience.

DAY TWENTY-TWO: THE LINKEDIN CHALLENGE

How is your LinkedIn game? Do you have a profile? If not, I really recommend that you do as LinkedIn is the perfect platform for building a network of contacts in your industry. Just to be clear, I'm not talking about building fans or super fans here, I'm talking about building the social proofing that allows you to grow your brand or business. If you have a new or dormant LinkedIn profile with no contacts, pictures or endorsements, you'll struggle to get traction. **Today's challenge is to set up a LinkedIn page if you don't already have one and if you do, your challenge is to work on building your social proofing.** What a lot of people don't realise about LinkedIn is that it's a media sharing platform. You can share blog posts and pictures and videos and ideas, all of which can be liked, engaged with and shared. What's really clever about LinkedIn is that, as it starts to figure out who you are and what you do, it will feature you and your content in relevant searches. Apparently this week, I've appeared in sixty-three LinkedIn searches. I had no idea until recently that this was a thing! LinkedIn is helping me get my name out there as a professional, so now I always share my social media content to LinkedIn and use it as part of my distribution. Spend a couple of hours today adding pictures and other content and relevant information about you to your page and start connecting with other professionals in your industry. Make yourself more findable and start to build that all important social proofing.

DAY TWENTY-THREE: THE THREE HOUR INSTA-BUILD CHALLENGE

Today, I want you to find three hours to look through your Instagram pictures and find the followers who like them the most. There will probably be thirty to fifty people who consistently like your Instagram content. **Today's challenge is to send each of these followers a personal message to say thank you for their support and let them know how much it means to you.**

DAY TWENTY-FOUR: THE DISTRIBUTION CHALLENGE

Today, I want to challenge you to get focused on distribution and create a potential network of people and places that could help promote your work. A great tip here is to come up with a list of people or companies who are working in the same field as you and search for reviews of them online. Now compile a second list of all the websites, blogs and vlogs that have reviewed them and their contact details. You need to start reaching out to these people, asking if they wouldn't mind taking a look at your product or service, with a view to reviewing it. These days everyone who's on social media is an influencer to some degree. Even someone with 200 followers on Instagram can still be a micro-influencer for your product or service.

A common excuse people come up with for not reaching out to influencers is that they think they won't have the time or space to feature them. If this is you, it really helps to look at things from the other point of view. For a year and a half I hosted a radio show on Juice with Ace from Skunk Anansie. The whole purpose of the show was to feature unsigned bands. We had to fill three hours of radio, four nights per week. This was a colossal amount of time. Every Monday I would panic, thinking, *what if we don't find enough bands to feature?* Whenever a band got in touch asking if we'd consider having them on the show I was so grateful. It's exactly the same with newspapers. Every day they have so much space to fill. It's relentless. And it's the same for vloggers and bloggers too. They're all trying to find new and exciting content to feature. So if you've been putting it off because you don't want to be a pain, you need to switch your thinking around and see how you would be helping them. The fact is, they probably need you just as much as you need them.

Today, make a list of bloggers, vloggers, podcasts, local and community radio stations, publications, reviewers and online influencers who can talk about you or invite you on to their show. Next, you need to come up with an angle; something that will make you stand out and make a good story. Instead of just saying 'we've got a new single out', tell them about the interesting backstory to the single or to you as a band, or come up with some kind of fun spin on a standard interview. We once featured a band called Your Very Own Flying Machine on our radio show and to make it stand out we challenged the bass player to punch the singer in the face live on air. The engagement we got on social media that night was more than we'd ever had before. People thought it was hilarious to do something so visual on radio and just hear the sound effects; the punch and yelp and cries of, 'Is he ok?' It was funny and silly and worked really well for our show. Not that I condone violence of course. OK, maybe I do in some situations but I appreciate that this kind of stunt might not be your cup of tea. The main point I'm making is to be creative in your approach so you capture people's imagination.

••••

DAY TWENTY-FIVE: THE INFLUENCER MARKETING CHALLENGE

Influencer marketing is simply asking someone else to give credibility and exposure to you or your product, or brand. You don't need to spend £100,000 trying to get an Instagram endorsement from the likes of Kim Kardashian. Every one of your friends has influence to some extent. **So, your challenge today is to find out what you can offer to get someone to promote you subtly on their page.** For example, if you take a screenshot of your band, single or album on Spotify and you send it to my Instagram there's a good chance I'll add it to my daily story, depending on how many I get. I do this for free but to get other people to do the same thing will be worth time, effort or money. Your job is to figure out how much time, effort or money you'd be prepared to pay for this exposure. Once you're clear on this, approach a bunch of relevant people (ie; people who appeal to your target demographic) and ask what you'd have to do for them to share a screenshot of you or your product on their Insta page or Story. Once they've responded, it's up to you whether you think this is a price worth paying.

DAY TWENTY-SIX: THE REWARD THE SUPER FAN CHALLENGE

A super-fan is the most important person in your entire audience because they engage with your content and spread the word about you and your work more than anyone else. **So today's challenge is for you to message your super-fans and give them something that will blow their fucking mind.** Thank them for their support and tell them how much they mean to you, then offer them something special as a way of showing your gratitude. It will make their day!

DAY TWENTY-SEVEN: THE REVERSE COLLAB CHALLENGE

Most people's first thought when it comes to collabs is, *how can I get in front of someone else's audience.* **But today I want you to think of collabs as a way of bringing value.** Flip it around and think of who you could get in front of your audience. This challenge is all about being the featurer, rather than the featured. Find a piece of content from someone else that you think your audience would love and share it with them, together with a message saying how much you like it. Your job is to give the other person 100% of the win, without expecting anything in return. If they do return the favour that's a bonus, but it's definitely not the point of today's exercise.

DAY TWENTY-EIGHT: THE FUTURE PLAN VIDEO CHALLENGE

Audiences need to know what their job is but most people get so caught up in creating content that they don't tell their followers what they'd like them to do. At a gig when the drummer hits the final cymbal of the song, the audience know it's time to cheer. Similarly, when the singer says, 'Everyone make some noise,' the audience knows exactly what to do. When it comes to social media, the same principle applies. Your audience are there for you and want to see more of you, it's your job to tell them what you'd like them to do – without taking advantage or being to salesy. **Today's challenge is to make a video, audio or written post bringing people up to speed with where you're at and how this affects them and what you'd like them to do.** Explain what you're working on and the timescales involved, then tell your followers what you'd like from them. If you're bringing them value and giving them a valid reason to take action, chances are they'll do what you want them to. For example, if you're in a band you could tell your followers that you're going to make an album and it's going to take three months and for those three months you're going to document the journey and include your followers in the key decisions because you want them to be a part of it. You could also tell your audience that you'd really value their feedback along the way. Once the album is released your target is to sell 1,000 copies and you'd really appreciate it if your audience could help you achieve this. Of course, many of your followers may not take part but a lot will and thanks to you setting things out clearly like this, they'll know exactly what to do.

DAY TWENTY-NINE: THE THANK YOU CHALLENGE

We're coming to the end of our 30 Day Challenge, **so today I want you to find a way to deliver a heart-warming thank you to your audience.** Tell them how grateful you are for their support and how much you appreciate it when they take the time to engage by leaving a comment or sharing a post. Make sure you reply to anyone who responds to your thank you. Taking the time to show your followers how much you value them is such a worthwhile investment.

DAY THIRTY: THE REVIEW CHALLENGE

We've come to the end of the 30 Day Challenge! **Your job for today is to go back through the entire 30 days and figure out what worked and what didn't.** What did you find easy? What did you find hard? What did your audience appreciate? And what did they ignore? Has the challenge made you discover any new skills? Make notes on each of the 30 days so that you can get clear on what works for you and what works for your audience and figure out how to combine the two. If you feel that you didn't get as much as you could have from the challenge because you just skimmed through, by all means go back and start again. Even if you didn't do it as thoroughly as you would have liked you will have learned something and you're bound to get more from it next time round. Remember, this is a long term investment in you and the way you develop your marketing. If you have taken this challenge seriously you'll be streets ahead of where you were a month ago and you'll have learned a lot about yourself and your audience. Now's the time to process all you've learned.

DAY THIRTY-ONE: BONUS CHALLENGE (BECAUSE WE BREAK THE RULES IN THIS HOUSE!)

With all the notes you've now got you're in the perfect position to design an ongoing social media strategy with pillars targets and a scheduled calendar that plays to your strengths and brings maximum value. You will no longer need to sit around waiting to be inspired or for the muse to strike. **Today's bonus challenge is to create a diary and allocate specific time slots for content research, creation, breakdown and distribution.** Use your findings from yesterday's review to guide you. From this point forward, there'll be no more uploading content and hoping for the best!

And finally...

Let's not forget that it wasn't long ago that I had zero social media experience and only one social media account, which was on Snapchat. I had no Facebook, no Instagram, no YouTube, just a need to bring value to a community. I am not your typical social media content provider, so if I can do this I have every belief that you can too – and probably a million times better! And if you've skipped to the back of the book to cut straight to the chase and find out the conclusion, here it is: **If you consistently provide valuable and unique content, love and support, and you're present in the room, you will win. Just be patient and keep showing up. Succeeding at social media is a marathon, not a sprint.**

ACKNOWLEDGEMENTS

Before the acknowledgements let's have some 'un-acknowledgements'. No thanks are due at all to the teachers who wrote me off, especially my science teachers, who wouldn't let me into classes and to my music teacher, who withdrew me from lessons! (If you've had a similar experience to this, I hope this book and my story inspires you to believe in yourself and go for your dreams. You only have one life – live it! Don't let anyone tell you you're not good enough.)

I would like to thank Siobhan Curham, who has been my writing coach and partner in this crazy book adventure. Considering that the last book I read was *Fantastic Mr Fox* (a great book by the way) I was excited but terrified at the prospect of writing a proper, real life book. Siobhan, thank you so much for your support, all of the hours put in and especially the biscuits – YUMMY! Now let's start planning book number 2, *The Rule Breakers Guide to Failure,* *spoiler alert!*

Also big thanks to John Michael Morgan, whose crazy brain-child this book is, your confidence in me is so appreciated.

To Bruce John Dickinson who believed in me when nobody else did, gave me a chance and mentored me for my entire life, I owe you everything and without you I would still be in the shampoo factory. Big love!

And to my team at DK management, who allow me to go on these crazy adventures. I love you all!

Thanks and love to my family, who have always believed in me even after several false starts and failures. Your support and regular boot up the arse has shaped who I am.

Thanks to Tom Heron for designing the cover image and understanding the line between offensive and fun way better than me! And to Matt Drew (www.mattdrew.co.uk), who has made this book into a real thing, with his amazing layout, production and design skills – even finding a way to start at THE END like I always do!

BOOK DAMIAN KEYES FOR YOUR NEXT EVENT

Damian Keyes has travelled the globe speaking at conferences, universities, company workshops and even in virtual reality! Damian has spent his entire life on stage performing, both as a musician and a keynote speaker, so he is completely at home with any crowd size. After all, how many people can say they shared the stage with Eric Clapton in front of 150,000 people?

Damian's funny but no nonsense style allows the audience to cut to the chase and learn invaluable insights into brand building. Damian isn't just inspirational, he's an instruction manual.

Here are a sample of the topics he speaks on:

The Rule Breaker's Guide to Social Media

Whatever the size or experience of your audience, Damian can tailor his keynote to your needs, ensuring multiple takeaways and an enjoyable talk. Over the past 20 years, Damian has built businesses worth over £60M and is an expert in marketing, branding and social media. Damian hasn't just watched this stuff on YouTube … he made it happen!

How to build an audience and what to do with them next

Today's technology allows us to build our own audience but how can you get noticed using nothing but creativity? And what do you do with your audience once you've got them?

How to break the rules to succeed

We are living in 'the creative age', where old rules no longer apply. In this talk Damian shows you how to get ahead using your skills, passion and dedication and he gets you to challenge any old beliefs that are holding you back.

Influencer marketing

Stop thinking that influencer marketing is for corporate household names only. With a bit of creativity and communication you can learn how to build your audience fast, using the power of free influencer marketing.

Whether it's a workshop or a keynote speech, Damian Keyes will engage and excite your audience, ensuring they leave full of energy and ready to tell the world how much they loved your event.

For more information visit: www.damiankeyes.com

And of course, you can find Damian all over social media at the following links:

Facebook.com/damokeyes
Instagram.com/damiankeyes1
YouTube.com/damiankeyes
Twitter.com/damiankeyes
Snapchat.com/damiankeyes
LinkedIn.com/damiankeyes

"Damian Keyes is as good a public speaker as I have ever seen. A life spent in business and performing means he owns the stage!" **Carol O'Leary, Starfish Entertainment**

Made in the USA
San Bernardino, CA
10 May 2020